INTRO TO iPHONE/iPAD APP DEVELOPMENT

STEP BY STEP TRAINING

Published by:
Noble Desktop LLC
594 Broadway, Suite 1202
New York, NY 10012
www.nobledesktop.com

Copyright © 2013 Noble Desktop LLC
Print Date: 11-5-2014
Revision: V.2014.11.05-20:22

All rights reserved. No part of this book may be reproduced or transmitted in any form by any means, electronic, mechanical, photocopy, recording, or otherwise without express written permission from the publisher. For information on reprint rights, please contact educator-in-chief@nobledesktop.com.

The publisher makes no representations or warranties with respect to the accuracy or completeness of the contents of this work, and specifically disclaims any warranties. Noble Desktop shall not have any liability to any person or entity with respect to any loss or damage caused or alleged to be caused directly or indirectly by the instructions contained in this book or by the computer software and hardware products described in it. Further, readers should be aware that software updates can make some of the instructions obsolete, and that websites listed in this work may have changed or disappeared since publication.

Adobe, the Adobe Logo, Creative Suite 6, InDesign, Illustrator, Photoshop, Dreamweaver, Flash, and Fireworks, are trademarks of Adobe Systems Incorporated.

Apple, Mac OS, and Macintosh are trademarks of Apple Inc. registered in the U.S. and other countries. Microsoft and Windows are either registered trademarks or trademarks of Microsoft Corporation in the U.S. and/or other countries. All other trademarks are the property of their respective owners.

This book was typeset using Linotype Syntax Pro and printed and bound in the United States of America.

INTRO TO iOS *Table of Contents*

SET UP & INTRODUCTION

How to Install Class Files 7

Before You Begin 9
    Topics Covered: Installing Xcode

STEP BY STEP EXERCISES

SECTION 1

EXERCISE 1A: Setting Up For Class: Do This Exercise First! 13
    Topics Covered: Setting Up Class Files

EXERCISE 1B: Hello World: Starting a Simple App 15
    Topics Covered: Creating a Single View Application
                        Getting to Know Xcode's Interface
                        Creating a Label and Button
                        Document Outline: View vs View Controller

EXERCISE 1C: Hello World: Making a Button Change Some Text 23
    Topics Covered: Assistant editor
                        ViewController.m vs .h
                        Creating an Outlet for the Text
                        Creating a Method for the Button
                        @synthesize
                        Testing the App in the iOS Simulator

EXERCISE 1D: Hello World: Clearing the Label 31
    Topics Covered: Using Xcode's Help
                        Removing the Initial Label Text
                        Conditional Logic
                        Method Calls

SECTION 2

EXERCISE 2A: Hello World: Intro to Objective-C 39
    Topics Covered: Creating a Class
                        Defining Properties
                        Error Alerts
                        Methods
                        @property Modifiers: strong/weak & nonatomic/atomic
                        @synthesize

Table of Contents INTRO TO iOS

EXERCISE 2B: Hello World: Finishing Up 45
  Topics Covered: Instantiation
    Creating Outlets
    Dot Notation vs. Getter and Setter Methods
    Placeholders for Values
    First Responder, Delegates & Dismissing the Keyboard
    Debugger Area and Breakpoints

EXERCISE 2C: Creating Simple Cells and Managing Retina Images 57
  Topics Covered: Adding Cells to the Table View
    Adding Images
    Adding Retina Images

SECTION 3

EXERCISE 3A: Building a Table View Controller 65
  Topics Covered: Creating a Class and Connecting it to the Storyboard
    Adding Properties for the Band Data
    Editing the Three DataSource Protocol Methods

EXERCISE 3B: The Navigation Controller 75
  Topics Covered: Navigation Controllers
    Setting the Initial View Controller
    Setting the Root View Controller
    Adding the Detail View Controller
    Segues

EXERCISE 3C: Creating the Band Detail View 81
  Topics Covered: Adding Label Objects
    Adding View Objects
    Changing Text Properties
    Adding a Divider Line
    Adding the Band Images

SECTION 4

EXERCISE 4A: Segues Part 1 91
  Topics Covered: What Is a Segue?
    prepareForSegue Method
    Band Detail Object

EXERCISE 4B: Segues Part 2: Passing Objects 99
  Topics Covered: NSMutableArray vs NSArray
    Creating a Mutable Array
    Connecting Band Detail Outlets in Code

EXERCISE 4C: Tab Bar Controller 107
  Topics Covered: Creating a Tab Bar Controller
    Using an Apple-Provided Tab Icon
    Using a Custom Tab Icon

INTRO TO iOS *Table of Contents*

EXERCISE 4D: Creating a Location Map 113
      Topics Covered: Adding the MapKit Framework
                      Adding a Map View
                      Setting a Specific Location on the Map
                      Defining Location Coordinates
                      Creating a Semi-Transparent Status Bar

SECTION 5

EXERCISE 5A: Linking to an External Webpage 123
      Topics Covered: Creating the Web View Controller
                      Coding the Link to the Webpage
                      Adding a Button Linking to the Webpage
                      Making the Webpage Scale to Fit

EXERCISE 5B: Embedding Video into the App 129
      Topics Covered: Adding a Video
                      Moving the Video to the Band Detail

EXERCISE 5C: Setting the Video for Each Band 135
      Topics Covered: Adding a videoURL Property
                      Defining videoURL for bandDetail Objects
                      stringWithFormat Method

EXERCISE 5D: Customizing the App for iPad 139
      Topics Covered: Creating a New iPad Storyboard
                      Setting the Interface Orientation

SECTION 6

EXERCISE 6A: Creating the Split View Controller 147
      Topics Covered: Adding a Split View Controller
                      Connecting and Reordering the View Controllers

EXERCISE 6B: Programming the Split View Controller 153
      Topics Covered: Connecting the Master and Detail View Controllers
                      Setting an Initial Detail View
                      Using the viewDidAppear Method

EXERCISE 6C: Fixing the iPad Layout 165
      Topics Covered: Fixing the Detail View for iPad
                      Finding Elements that Seem to Have Disappeared

EXERCISE 6D: App Settings: Icons & Launch Images 169
      Topics Covered: Preparing the Assets
                      Adding App Icons & Launch Images

Table of Contents INTRO TO iOS

REFERENCE MATERIAL

Submitting to the App Store 177
        Topics Covered: Enrolling in the iOS Developer Program
                          Provisioning Your Devices For Testing and Deployment
                          Creating iTunes Record
                          Submitting & Releasing Your App

App Icon & Launch Image File Names & Sizes 181

Objective-C Programming: Basic Terms & Concepts 183

INTRO TO iOS *How to Install Class Files*

INSTALLATION

Thank you for purchasing a Noble Desktop Course Workbook!

These instructions tell you how to install the class files used in this workbook.

DOWNLOADING & INSTALLING CLASS FILES

1. Navigate to the **Desktop**.

2. Create a **new folder** called **Class Files** (this is where you'll put the files after they have been downloaded).

3. Go to **nobledesktop.com/download**

4. Enter the code **ios-intro-1411-05**

5. If you haven't already click **Start Download**.

6. After the **.zip** file has finished downloading, be sure to unzip the file if it hasn't been done for you. You should end up with a **iOS Intro Class** folder.

7. Drag the downloaded folder into the **Class Files** folder you just made. These are the files you will use while going through the workbook.

8. If you still have the downloaded .zip file you can delete that.

   That's it! Enjoy.

INTRO TO iOS *Before You Begin*

INSTALLING XCODE

Xcode requires a Mac running OS 10.8.4 Mountain Lion or later. If you have an older system, you'll have to upgrade to run Xcode. Windows users cannot run Xcode. You must have a Mac to use it and go through this workbook.

Xcode is over 2 GB, so it may take a while to download depending on the speed of your internet connection.

1. On your Mac, launch the **App Store** (in the **Applications** folder).

2. At the top right of the window, search for **Xcode.**

3. In the search results, next to **Xcode,** click the **Free** button. (If it says **Installed** you already have Xcode, and can skip this step and the following step.)

4. The button will turn into a green **Install App** button. Click **Install App** and follow any further instructions, such as logging in with your Apple ID.

5. After it's installed, launch **Xcode** (in the **Applications** folder). The first time you run Xcode you may be required to install a system component as well as agree to their terms, so go ahead and do that now.

INTRO TO iOS

Section Topics
SECTION 1

SETTING UP FOR CLASS: DO THIS EXERCISE FIRST!
Setting Up Class Files

HELLO WORLD: STARTING A SIMPLE APP
Creating a Single View Application
Getting to Know Xcode's Interface
Creating a Label and Button
Document Outline: View vs. View Controller

HELLO WORLD: MAKING A BUTTON CHANGE SOME TEXT
Assistant editor
ViewController.m vs. .h
Creating an Outlet for the Text
Creating a Method for the Button
@synthesize
Testing the App in the iOS Simulator

HELLO WORLD: MAKING LABEL INITIALLY BLANK
Using Xcode's Help
Removing the Initial Label Text
Conditional Logic
Method Calls

INTRO TO iOS *Setting Up For Class: Do This Exercise First!*

SETTING UP YOUR OWN COPY OF CLASS FILES

Throughout this workbook, you will be editing class files that we have prepared for you. Instead of editing the originals, we'll have you make a copy just for you to edit.

1. **Download the class files.** Refer to the instructions on page 7 on how to download and install the class files.

2. On the **Desktop**, open the **Class Files** folder.

3. Click once on the **iOS Intro Class** folder to select it.

4. Press **Cmd–D** to duplicate it.

5. Rename the duplicate folder **yourname-iOS Intro Class**.

   You now have your own set of class files to use throughout the class. Have fun!

INTRO TO iOS *Hello World: Starting a Simple App*

EXERCISE PREVIEW

EXERCISE OVERVIEW

In the next few exercises, you'll create a very simple app that will change some text when you tap a button. In this exercise you'll start learning the Xcode interface and create the text and button. Later exercises will add the logic to make the button work and actually change that text. Let's first see how to add the basic elements to the screen.

GETTING STARTED

1. Launch **Xcode** (it's in the **Applications** folder). If you do not currently have Xcode installed on your Mac, refer to the **Setup** section earlier in this workbook for installation instructions.

2. If you see the **Welcome to Xcode** window, on the lefthand side, click on **Create a new Xcode project.** If you don't see the **Welcome to Xcode** window, go to **File > New > Project (Cmd–Shift–N).**

3. We'll start off simple and use a basic starter template. In the categories on the left, under **iOS** make sure **Application** is selected.

4. On the right side, double–click on the **Single View Application** template.

5. Set the following:
   – Product Name: **HelloWorld**
   – Organization Name: **Noble Desktop**
   – Company Identifier: **com.nobledesktop**
   – Class Prefix: (leave blank)
   – Devices: **iPhone**

6. Click **Next.**

NOBLE DESKTOP — STEP BY STEP TRAINING — NOBLEDESKTOP.COM   PAGE 15

Hello World: Starting a Simple App **INTRO TO iOS**

7. You'll now be asked where you want to save the project. Navigate into the **Desktop > Class Files > yourname-iOS Intro Class** folder.

8. Check **Create git repository on My Mac** if it is not already checked. (This can be used to track changes you make over time.)

9. Click **Create** to finish specifying the location of the new Xcode project.

10. You should now see a summary of general information is listed about your app. Most of it is used in the final stages of app development, when you're ready to deploy your app to the App Store. First things first—let's start developing this app!

STORYBOARD, VIEW CONTROLLER, & OBJECT LIBRARY

1. The section found on the far left is called the **Project Navigator.**

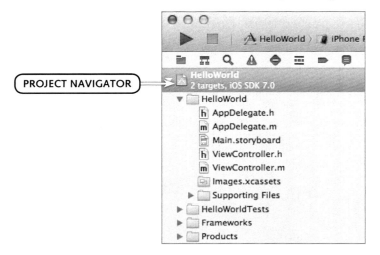

2. In the **Project Navigator,** you'll find a list of files Xcode created for us. It's still too early in your app-developing endeavours to be burdened by these files' intricacies, but in a nutshell:

    - **AppDelegate:** entry point for the application
    - **Main.storyboard:** visual representation of the app
    - **ViewController:** where you'll put the code associated with the storyboard's visuals
    - **Images.xcassets:** asset catalog used to manage images in the app

    You will get more comfortable with these relationships as you work with them throughout this book.

3. In the **Project Navigator's** list of files, click on **Main.storyboard.**

INTRO TO iOS *Hello World: Starting a Simple App*

1B EXERCISE

4. Let's get to know Xcode's interface a bit better. It is divided into several areas. These areas are not labelled onscreen, so we've labelled them below the screenshot so you can start to learn their names. If you don't see a particular section, don't worry you'll soon learn how to show and hide them.

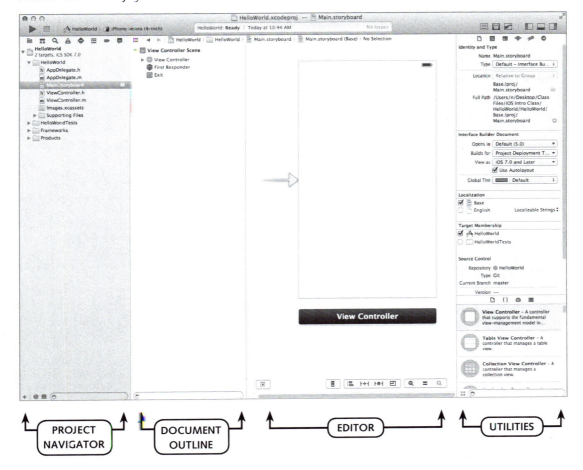

PROJECT NAVIGATOR   DOCUMENT OUTLINE   EDITOR   UTILITIES

5. The main center area is the **Editor**. This is where you will view and edit the contents of files. The column to the right of the **Project Navigator** (second column from the left) is the **Document Outline**. If you do not see this column, at the bottom left of the **Editor** area, click the **Show Document Outline** button (▶) to show it.

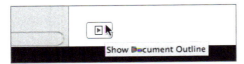

6. The column on the righthand side of the window is the **Utilities** area, which includes **object libraries** and **inspectors** to set options.

Hello World: Starting a Simple App INTRO TO iOS

7. You can hide or show the **Projector Navigator** and **Utilities** areas using the **View** buttons at the top right of the window.

8. If you've been experimenting with showing and hiding areas, make sure that you see all four areas: **Project Navigator, Document Outline, Editor** and **Utilities.**

9. In the **Document Outline** area (second from left, the column to the right of Project Navigator) click on **View Controller** (you may have to expand **View Controller Scene** to see it).

10. Towards the bottom right of the window (which is the bottom of the **Utilities** area) click on the **Object library** tab (🗔) to see various objects we can use:

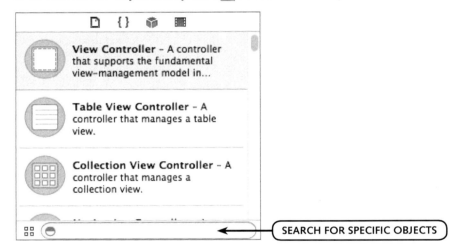

NOTE: Xcode provides us with many pre-made objects that can be inserted directly onto the View.

11. Scroll through the list of objects to see some of the items available to us.

12. We want to find the **Button.** Instead of scrolling through the long list to find it, at the bottom there's a search field. In the search field type **button** to filter the list. Now you only see objects with button in their name.

INTRO TO iOS *Hello World: Starting a Simple App*

13. Drag the **Button** from the **Object library** onto the center of the **View** in the **Editor** area, as shown below. Use the blue horizontal and vertical guides that automatically appear to center the button exactly.

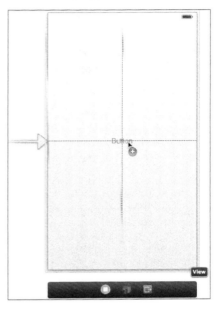

NOTE: Sometimes when you first pull an object out of the library, Xcode will take a moment to respond. If you don't see the object appear on the view right away, just keep holding down the mouse button and wait until Xcode catches up with you.

14. In the **Object library** change the search to **label**

15. From the **Object library,** drag a **Label** onto the **View** in the **Editor**. Center it above the button, as shown below.

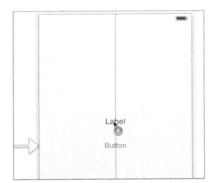

16. Changing the text of the label and button is easy. Double–click on the **Label.**

17. Change the text to **I am going to change** and press **Return** to finish editing.

18. Double–click on the **Button.**

19. Change the text to **Change the Text** and press **Return** to finish editing.

20. You'll notice that in both cases the button's container expands automatically to match the additional text.

21. The elements are no longer centered. To re-center them, select each object and move them back to their original positions, as indicated by the blue guides.

Hello World: Starting a Simple App INTRO TO iOS

1B EXERCISE

INSPECTORS

Right now the only difference between our label and button is the text color. Let's style the button to distinguish it from our label.

1. In the Editor area, select the **Change the Text** button.

2. On the right side of the window (at the top of the **Utilities** area), find the **Inspector selector bar** (shown below):

   These various inspectors allow you to look at and change different attributes.

3. Click on the **Attributes inspector** tab ( ).

   The Attributes inspector has many options for styling the appearance of objects (font, color, etc.). Notice that under Title, you can see the text for our button.

4. Scroll down to the View options and set **Background** to **Light Gray Color**. (Click on the word **Default** rather than the color rectangle.)

5. Under the Button options further up, set the following:

   Text Color: **White Color**
   Inset, Top and Bottom: **8**
   Inset, Left and Right: **15**

6. The changes to the inset margin cropped off some of our text. To set a custom width, click on the **Size inspector** tab ( ).

   The Size inspector is useful for precisely specifying dimensions and other attributes of objects.

7. Let's give the button a custom, larger width. We want the button to remain centered, so before we change the width, let's set the **Origin**. As shown to the right, click the **center** origin point.

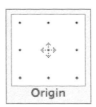
Origin

8. Now when we change the width, the button will remain centered.
   Above **Width,** change the value to **200** and press **Return.**

9. While it's nice to know that we can set a custom width, let's set it back to an auto width that's determined by the content. In the Editor, click outside the iPhone screen to deselect the button.

10. Click on the button to reselect it.

11. Go into **Editor > Size to Fit Content.** (While **Edit > Undo** would do the same in this case, we wanted you to know where this command is located.)

12. Drag the button back to the center of the screen.

INTRO TO iOS *Hello World: Starting a Simple App*

1B EXERCISE

13. Click on the **Connections inspector** tab ( ).

    The Connections inspector gives you control over what occurs on certain events. Essentially, it creates relationships between objects. Right now, you won't see any connections because we haven't made any yet. We'll do that later.

THE DOCUMENT OUTLINE

1. In the **Editor** area, click on the iPhone screen (the View).

2. Let's examine the **Document Outline** (the column to the right of the Project Navigator):

    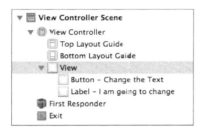

    This gives us a representation of each object that is in our Storyboard Editor.

3. In the **Document Outline**, notice the following are inside the View:

    - Button – Change the Text
    - Label – I am going to change

4. In the **Document Outline,** click on **View.**

5. In the Editor, notice the iPhone screen is highlighted light blue. That's because the View object represents the entire visual area of the iOS device's screen.

6. In the **Document Outline,** click on **View Controller.**

Hello World: Starting a Simple App INTRO TO iOS

7. In the Editor, notice the **status bar** with the **battery** (▬) on top, the **View** below that, and **controller** at the bottom are all outlined in blue. The **View's** parent class is the **View Controller,** which is a controller object. The View Controller corresponds to its header file (ViewController.h) and its implementation file (ViewController.m) listed in the Project Navigator. We'll learn more about these starting in the next exercise.

8. Do a **File > Save.**

9. Leave the project open. In the next exercise we'll link up the button so when you click it, it will change the label's text.

INTRO TO iOS *Hello World: Making a Button Change Some Text*

1C EXERCISE

EXERCISE PREVIEW

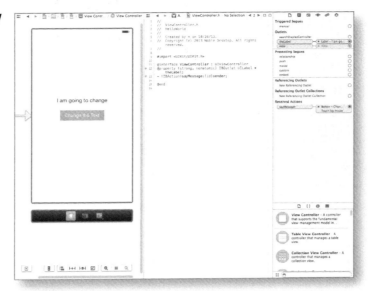

EXERCISE OVERVIEW

In the previous exercise we created a label and button. When the user taps the button, we want it to change the label's text. That's what we'll program in this exercise.

THE ASSISTANT EDITOR

1. If you did not complete the previous exercises (1A–1B), complete them now before starting this exercise.

2. **HelloWorld.xcodeproj** should still be open from the previous exercise. If you closed it, re-open as follows:

   – Go to **File > Open**.
   – Navigate to **Desktop > Class Files > yourname-iOS Intro Class > HelloWorld** and double–click on **HelloWorld.xcodeproj**.

3. In the Project Navigator make sure **Main.storyboard** is selected.

4. Currently, you should be in the Standard editor, but it would be helpful if we could see the code and its visual side-by-side. Let's switch into the Assistant editor to do this. First, we need to make room on the screen for two panes. In the bottom left of the Editor, click the **Hide Document Outline** (▢) button.

5. Because the Assistant editor will show code associated with the selection, make sure the **View Controller** is selected in the Editor area. At the top of the **View Controller** click the **battery** (▬) so that the whole controller is highlighted in blue.

Hello World: Making a Button Change Some Text INTRO TO iOS

6. At the top right of the window, notice the **Editor** toolbar ( ).

7. Click on the middle icon to **Show the Assistant editor** ( ).

   NOTE: If the **Document Outline** pops out again, it's a glitch, and you should just set it back to **Standard editor** ( ) and re-try these steps.

8. Now we have an area for the View and an area for the code. Adjust the size of the sections so that you have a layout similar to the screenshot below:

FORGING BONDS

1. Now the code for **ViewController.m** (implementation file) is open on the right.

   All the programming logic needs to be coded in the **implementation file (ViewController.m).**

2. Notice that ViewController.m **imports** the header file:
   ```
   #import "ViewController.h"
   ```
   .m and .h files work together. A .m file always imports the associated .h file. **Header** files always end with .h and **implementation** files end with .m

3. Let's take a look at the header file. At the top of the code on the right side of the Editor, click **ViewController.m** to reveal a menu that looks like this:

4. Select **ViewController.h** to go into the header file.

INTRO TO iPHONE/iPAD APP DEVELOPMENT

INTRO TO iOS *Hello World: Making a Button Change Some Text*

1C EXERCISE

In Objective-C, a **header file** (like ViewController.h) contains declarations of variables and methods. It does NOT contain any programming logic that specifically defines what the methods or variables do within the program.

If we want to control an object in the View (like changing the text of our label) there has to be an **outlet** property associated with it in the code in the header file. Fortunately, there's an easy way to insert outlets into the code from the Editor. We want to control the label we created in the previous exercise, so let's start with that.

5. In the Editor, hold the **Control** key and drag the **Label** to the ViewController.h code underneath this line:

   `@interface ViewController : UIViewController`

   A blue line will appear under this code line, as shown below. When you see it, release the mouse.

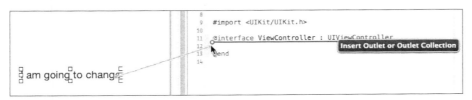

   NOTE: If you have a two-button mouse (or an Apple Magic Mouse set to work as two buttons) you don't have to hold Control. Instead, you drag with the **Right** mouse button instead of the left button. So either a **Right mouse button–drag** or a **Control–drag** will let you make the connection line.

6. In the prompt that appears set the following:
   – Name: **theLabel**
      (Pay attention to upper versus lowercase. Programming is case-sensitive!)

   – Storage: **Strong**
      (Storage will be explained more in a later exercise, but typically we'll use Strong because as long as this view exists, we want this label to exist. We're creating a strong relationship between the two.)

7. Click **Connect** (or hit **Return**).

   NOTE: Creating an outlet (what we just did) names our label object "theLabel". The variable in the code (it is black) corresponds to the label on the View.

8. You just automatically inserted this line of code into ViewController.h!

   `@property (strong, nonatomic) IBOutlet UILabel *theLabel;`

   NOTE: For now try not to be intimidated by the syntax—in time (and with practice) it will make sense. The **IB** in IBOutlet stands for **Interface Builder.**

9. But, does the Storyboard also know about this connection? Let's find out. In the Editor make sure the **Label** is selected.

1C EXERCISE

Hello World: Making a Button Change Some Text INTRO TO iOS

10. At the top right of the window, click on the **Connections inspector** tab ( ).

11. In the **Referencing Outlets** section, notice that the **theLabel** attribute is associated with the View Controller object:

12. In theory, the **Button** has not yet been coded, so it should not be associated with the View Controller object yet. To confirm this, in the Editor, click on the **Button.**

13. In the **Connections inspector** ( ), notice that we don't have any such association as of yet, because we haven't even named the object.

CREATING A METHOD FOR THE BUTTON

We want to create a button that the user can tap and change the text. Instead of associating an outlet, we need to create a method which responds to an event (such as the user tapping the button).

1. As shown below, in the Editor, **Right mouse button–drag** or **Control–drag** from the **Button** to the **ViewController.h** code. Release underneath the **@property** code:

2. In the prompt that appears, set:
   – Connection: **Action**
   – Name: **sayMessage**
   – Event: **Touch Up Inside**

   NOTE: The **Event** field asks for the exact action that needs to take place before the **sayMessage:** method is called. **Touch Up Inside** means the user must "touch and release" the button rather than just "touch" it for a moment.

3. Leave the rest as is and click **Connect** (or hit **Return**).

4. In the ViewController.h code, notice that a method called **sayMessage:** has been added after the **property** code.

   `- (IBAction)sayMessage:(id)sender;`

   NOTE: For now try not to be intimidated by the syntax—in time (and with practice) it will make sense. The **IB** in IBAction stands for **Interface Builder.**

PAGE 26   INTRO TO iPHONE/iPAD APP DEVELOPMENT

INTRO TO iOS *Hello World: Making a Button Change Some Text*

5. In the Editor, make sure the **Button** is selected.

6. On the right side of the window, in the **Connections inspector** (⊙), under **Sent Events,** notice that **Touch Up Inside** is linked to the ViewController method **sayMessage:**.

PROGRAMMING IN THE IMPLEMENTATION FILE

1. In the Project Navigator's list of files on the left, select **ViewController.m** to view its code.

   Its code will open on the left, where the Storyboard used to be.

2. Remember how dragging the **Button** from the Editor to the header file added some code for us? Well, it also started us off in the implementation file. Towards the bottom of the code, find the related code that was inserted:

   ```
   - (IBAction)sayMessage:(id)sender {
   }
   ```

3. Add the following line of code shown below in **bold.** Don't forget the semi-colon at the end!

   ```
   - (IBAction)sayMessage:(id)sender {
       theLabel.text = @"It worked!";
   }
   ```

   Let's dissect this new line of code. First of all, Xcode has built-in objects. For example, **theLabel** (which we created earlier) is a **UILabel** object. All objects prefixed with the letters **UI** are provided to us by Xcode. **UILabel** objects have attributes and methods, and **theLabel** inherited all of them. We can override them if needed. One of **UILabel's** attributes is **text.** The above code accesses **theLabel's** text attribute and assigns it the string "It worked!". (A string is a series of characters.)

4. Notice there's an error in the code, as indicated by the **red error** icon (⊙) to the left of the code:

   ```
       // Dispose of any resources that can be recreated.
   }

   - (IBAction)sayMessage:(id)sender {
       theLabel.text = @"It worked!";
   }
   @end
   ```

5. Click on that **red error** icon (⊙) and an error message will pop up.

   NOTE: If you accidentally clicked on the column and a **breakpoint** (▭) appears, drag it off that column to remove it. (We'll discuss breakpoints in the future.)

Hello World: Making a Button Change Some Text INTRO TO iOS

6. After clicking the **red error** icon (⬤), a message will appear saying, **"Use of undeclared identifier 'theLabel'..."**

So, what went wrong? Basically, the method doesn't know what the object **theLabel** is, because we've forgotten to give the **method** access to the **variable.** In other words, we've forgotten to give **sayMessage** access to **theLabel.**

7. To fix this, we'll use **@synthesize**. Find the following line of code:

```
@implementation ViewController
```

NOTE: Be careful not to confuse this with the **@interface** line near the top. Be sure to find the **@implementation** line a few lines below that!

8. Below that, add the following bold code:

```
@implementation ViewController
@synthesize theLabel;
```

@synthesize tells Xcode to create automatic methods for theLabel, called **getter** and **setter** methods, so that other parts of the code can use **theLabel,** as well as its variables. Getters and setters are used in object-oriented programming (OOP) to get and set object property values. That's what we're doing in this app, getting a string of text and then setting the label equal to that text.

NOTE: In newer versions of Xcode, @synthesize is no longer required in most cases as it will be provided by default. Now you only need the @property directive and Xcode takes care of synthesizing (creating getter and setter methods) for you. By default, if we hadn't added the @synthesize line to our code, we could get access to theLabel by either including an underscore at the beginning (_theLabel) or prefixing the reference with self (self.theLabel). As you work on older projects, you'll see it's standard practice to declare a property, then add the @synthesize code, which is how this book was written. In newer versions, while @synthesize isn't necessary in most cases, using it just changes the name which you refer to properties by. So in our code instead of using the default _theLabel, because we used @synthesize, we can just use theLabel.

9. At the top right of Xcode's window, switch to the **Standard editor** (📋).

TESTING THE APP

1. At the top left of the window is the **Scheme** (shown below).

PAGE 28   INTRO TO iPHONE/iPAD APP DEVELOPMENT

INTRO TO iOS *Hello World: Making a Button Change Some Text*

2. Make sure it is set to **HelloWorld > iPhone Retina (4-inch)**. If it's set to another type of device (such as iPad), click on that menu and choose **iPhone Retina (4-inch)**.

3. At the top left of the window, click on the **Run** button (▶).
   This compiles the code and opens the **iOS Simulator** app.

   NOTE: If you get a prompt asking if you want to **Enable Developer Mode,** click **Enable**. It will ask for the admin username and password. If you're in a class, have the instructor enter the password.

4. It may take a little while to launch, but eventually, the iOS Simulator will appear (shown to the right).

   NOTE: If the iOS Simulator is too big (you have to scroll to see the entire view), go into **Window > Scale** and choose an option that fits your display.

5. In the iOS Simulator, click the **Change the Text** button. The label's text should change. The text "It worked!" shows up, but it is not centered.

6. Let's fix that. Switch back to Xcode and click the **Stop** button (■).

7. In the Project Navigator, click on **Main.storyboard**.

8. Click on the label that says **I am going to change**.

9. In the Utilities, click on the **Attributes inspector** tab ( ).

10. Under **Alignment**, click the **Center Align** button (≡) to center the text.

11. Let's try this again. Click on the **Run** button (▶).

12. In the iOS Simulator, click the **Change the Text** button. The label's text should change. The text stayed centered this time. Woohoo, you've created your first iOS app!

13. Switch back to Xcode and click the **Stop** button (■).

14. Do a **File > Save**.

15. Leave the project open. We'll continue to work on it in the next exercise.

INTRO TO iOS *Hello World: Clearing the Label*

EXERCISE PREVIEW

EXERCISE OVERVIEW

In the previous exercise we made a button change some text. In this exercise you'll learn how to hide the initial text, so users don't see it until they tap the button. After they tap the button, the text will appear. We'll also make it so the button toggles between displaying the text and clearing the text.

1. If you did not complete the previous exercises (1A–1C), complete them now before starting this exercise.

2. **HelloWorld.xcodeproj** should still be open from the previous exercise. If you closed it, re-open as follows:

   – Go to **File > Open**.
   – Navigate to **Desktop > Class Files > yourname–iOS Intro Class > HelloWorld** and double–click on **HelloWorld.xcodeproj**.

SEARCHING XCODE'S HELP

Xcode's documentation provides definitions of the classes and objects offered to you. If you ever need to know an object's or class' attributes or methods, you will unquestionably find yourself using this time after time. Let's take a look.

1. Go to **Help > Documentation and API Reference**.

Hello World: Clearing the Label INTRO TO iOS

1D EXERCISE

2. Xcode automatically created a class called **ViewController,** whose attributes and methods are inherited from its superclass **UIViewController.** Let's see what the help tells us about this class. Into the search field at the top, type **UIViewController** and wait a moment for the results to appear.

3. Click on the first result (which should be for **UIViewController**).

4. Scroll down to the **Overview** section.

   Here you see a summary of the class. You don't have to read it now, but this will give you a sense of what this class does. The UIViewController class is the core foundation for any iOS app. It lets you represent each screen.

5. To the left of the document in the table of contents click on the **Tasks** section to see a list of methods available to this class.

6. Under **Managing the View** click on **viewDidLoad.** Here we can see a description of **viewDidLoad** and when this method is called.

   The main thing to understand is that every time a View Controller is instantiated, there are a series of methods that are called to build that View. Most of the View is already built for us, so some methods have already been called for us.

7. Close the Documentation window.

8. In the Project Navigator click on **ViewController.m** to open it.

9. Find the `- (void)viewDidLoad` method.

   As we read earlier, it is one of the methods that was automatically called, and it already does a lot, but let's add a little more to its functionality.

INITIALLY BLANK LABEL

1. Let's set the initial label text to be blank upon loading. We'll use the viewDidLoad method because it is automatically called after the View Controller has loaded. As shown below, add the following bold code:

   ```
   - (void)viewDidLoad
   {
       [super viewDidLoad];
       // Do any additional setup after loading the view, typically from a nib.
       theLabel.text = @"";
   }
   ```

2. Press **Cmd–S** to save.

3. In the top-left corner of the toolbar, click on the **Run** (▶) button **(Cmd–R)**.

   NOTE: If you get a warning asking if you want to **Stop "Hello World"**, click **Stop.**

4. Bam! After the **iOS Simulator** loads, you see that the label appears hidden initially, because its text attribute is blank.

PAGE 32 INTRO TO iPHONE/iPAD APP DEVELOPMENT

INTRO TO iOS *Hello World: Clearing the Label*

1D EXERCISE

5. In the **iOS Simulator,** click the **Button** to see the new text is displayed.

6. Switch back to Xcode.

7. Click the **Stop** button (■).

CONDITIONAL LOGIC

Let's add a little more functionality to our button. When the user clicks the button again, let's make it so it clears the text. To do this we need to add some logic to our button that says if the initial label is blank, change it to "It worked!", but if the label says, "It worked!" change it so it is blank.

1. Find the following block of code for our button (starting around line 31):

   ```
   - (IBAction)sayMessage:(id)sender {
       theLabel.text = @"It worked!";
   }
   ```

2. Add the following code shown below in **bold:**

   ```
   - (IBAction)sayMessage:(id)sender {
       if(){

       }else{

       }
       theLabel.text = @"It worked!";
   }
   ```

   The code you just added is a basic if/else statement. Inside the parentheses is where you put the condition you want to test. If that's true it runs the code you add in the brackets that follow. If is isn't (else) it runs the code in the brackets after else.

3. Let's have our if statement test to see if theLabel's text is already set to "It worked!" Add the following bold code:

   ```
   - (IBAction)sayMessage:(id)sender {
       if([theLabel.text isEqualToString:@"It worked!"]){

       }else{
   ```

   The code you just added checks to see if theLabel's text is equal to "It worked!" It does this by calling the isEqualToString: method on theLabel.text. As you can guess from the name, the isEqualToString: method checks to see if a string is equal to the string you specify.

4. If theLabel's text is "It worked!" we want theLabel's text to be blank. Add the following bold code:

   ```
   - (IBAction)sayMessage:(id)sender {
       if([theLabel.text isEqualToString:@"It worked!"]){
           theLabel.text = @"";
       }else{

       }
       theLabel.text = @"It worked!";
   }
   ```

NOBLE DESKTOP — STEP BY STEP TRAINING — NOBLEDESKTOP.COM

1D EXERCISE — Hello World: Clearing the Label INTRO TO iOS

5. If theLabel's text is NOT already set to "It worked!" we want to set it to that. Cut the line of code that sets theLabel's text to "It worked!" and paste it into the else statement brackets so the final code looks like this:

    ```
    - (IBAction)sayMessage:(id)sender {
      if([theLabel.text isEqualToString:@"It worked!"]){
          theLabel.text = @"";
      }else{
          theLabel.text = @"It worked!";
      }
    }
    ```

6. In the top-left corner of the toolbar, click on the **Run** (▶) button **(Cmd–R)**.

7. After the **iOS Simulator** loads, click the **Button** to see the "It worked!" text is displayed.

8. Click the Button again to clear the text. Awesome! However, let's make it so instead of the button saying Change the Text, it toggles between saying Display the Text and Clear the Text.

9. Switch back to Xcode.

10. Click the **Stop** button (■).

CHANGING THE BUTTON TEXT

1. In the Project Navigator click on **Main.storyboard.**

2. Double–click on the **Change the Text** button text.

3. Change the text to **Display the Text** and press **Return** to finish editing.

4. In the Project Navigator click on **ViewController.m** to open it.

5. Find the following block of code for our button:

    ```
    - (IBAction)sayMessage:(id)sender {
      if([theLabel.text isEqualToString:@"It worked!"]){
          theLabel.text = @"";
      }else{
          theLabel.text = @"It worked!";
      }
    }
    ```

6. In order to change the button's text we have to use the **setTitle:forState:** method on the button. Add the following bold code:

    ```
    - (IBAction)sayMessage:(id)sender {
       if([theLabel.text isEqualToString:@"It worked"]){
           theLabel.text = @"";
       }else{
           theLabel.text = @"It worked!";
           [sender setTitle:@"Clear the Text" forState:UIControlStateNormal];
       }
    }
    ```

INTRO TO iOS *Hello World: Clearing the Label*

1D EXERCISE

This code is similar to the code we used earlier to determine if theLabel's text was equal to a specific string in that they are both method calls. Here we call the setTitle:forState: method on sender (our button that triggered this action). The method takes two parameters, the text you are setting the title to, and the state of the button you are changing the text for. A button has different states. We want to change the text of the button when it is normal (not pressed) so we use UIControlStateNormal. There are other states, such as UIContro StateHighlighted, for when a button is pressed.

7. Let's try this out. In the top-left corner of the toolbar, click on the **Run** button (▶) or hit **Cmd–R.**

8. After the iOS Simulator loads, click the **Button** to see the button's text changes to **Clear the Text.** Sweet!

9. Click the **Button** again to clear the text. Notice that the button keeps saying Clear the Text. Let's fix that.

10. Switch back to Xcode.

11. Add the following bold code to change the button back to Display the Text when it clears the text:

    ```
    - (IBAction)sayMessage:(id)sender {
        if([theLabel.text isEqualToString:@"It worked!"]){
            theLabel.text = @"";
            [sender setTitle:@"Display the Text" forState:UIControlStateNormal];
        }else{
            theLabel.text = @"It worked!";
            [sender setTitle:@"Clear the Text" forState:UIControlStateNormal];
        }
    }
    ```

12. In the top-left corner of the toolbar, click on the **Run** (▶) button **(Cmd–R).**

    NOTE: If you get a warning asking if you want to **Stop "Hello World",** click **Stop.**

13. After the iOS Simulator loads click the **Button** to see the button's text changes to Clear the Text.

14. Click the **Button** again to clear the text. Notice that the button now says Display the Text. Fantastic!

15. Switch back to Xcode.

16. Click the **Stop** button (■).

17. Do a **File > Save.**

18. Leave the project open. We'll continue to work on it in the next exercise.

INTRO TO iOS

Section Topics
SECTION 2

INTRO TO OBJECTIVE-C
Creating a Class
Defining Properties
Error Alerts
Methods
@property Modifiers: strong/weak & nonatomic/atomic
@synthesize

HELLO WORLD: FINISHING UP
Instantiation
Creating Outlets
Dot Notation vs. Getter and Setter Methods
Placeholders for Values
First Responder, Delegates & Dismissing the Keyboard
Debugger Area and Breakpoints

CREATING SIMPLE CELLS AND MANAGING RETINA IMAGES
Adding Cells to the Table View
Adding Images
Adding Retina Images

INTRO TO iOS *Hello World: Intro to Objective-C*

2A EXERCISE

EXERCISE PREVIEW

EXERCISE OVERVIEW

In this exercise, you will learn some of the basic foundations of Objective-C and programming so that you will better understand future exercises. Some of the mystique of programming in any language goes away by learning two things: the correct **terminology** (or vocabulary) and the **syntax**. Some of the most basic terms you need to know are Object and Class. Objective-C is called an **Object-Oriented Programming** language. An **Object** is used to represent things. You can also think of it as a noun (such as a button). You make an Object by creating a new file called a Class. You can think of a **Class** as a template from which you create objects.

1. If you did not complete the previous exercises (1A–1D), complete them now before starting this exercise.

2. **HelloWorld.xcodeproj** should still be open from the previous exercise. If you closed it, re-open as follows:

   – Go to **File > Open**.
   – Navigate to **Desktop > Class Files > yourname-iOS Intro Class > HelloWorld** and double–click on **HelloWorld.xcodeproj**.

CREATING A CLASS

1. Classes are defined in files, so let's create those files now. In the Project Navigator select **ViewController.m**. (We want the new file to be added after this file, that's why we had you select it.)

2. Go to **File > New > File**.

3. On the left, under **iOS** select **Cocoa Touch**.

4. Double–click on **Objective-C class** to choose it.

5. From the **Subclass of** menu choose **NSObject** (or start typing it and let Xcode autocomplete it for you).

2A EXERCISE

Hello World: Intro to Objective-C INTRO TO iOS

NSObject is the most basic object we can use as a parent. Our class will be a child of the parent. Children inherit the functionality of the parent. Though a parent is not required, NSObject gives us a lot of built-in functionality to make it easier for iOS app programming. **NS** stands for **NeXTSTEP**. NeXT was the company Steve Jobs went on to create after being ousted from Apple. NeXTSTEP was NeXT's operating system. When Apple bought NeXT, they got Steve Jobs back and NeXTSTEP became the foundation for Mac OS X, which later became the foundation for iOS.

6. For **Class** type **Person**
7. Click **Next**.
8. You should already be in the **HelloWorld** folder, so click **Create**.
9. In the Project Navigator notice **Person.h** and **Person.m** have been added. Those two files make up the **Person** Class.
   - **Person.h** is a header file containing declarations of our variables and methods.
   - **Person.m** is an implementation file containing the logic within our methods.

DEFINING PROPERTIES

A **Property** represents the characteristics of an Object. For example, our Person class could contain properties that specify name, height, address, etc. In addition to defining the characteristics of an Object, a Property also maintains the state.

As we add properties, we'll start talking about the syntax of writing code in Objective-C. Every programming language has a syntax. Similar to a spoken language, which uses punctuation to help define a particular meaning, a programming language syntax will use symbols in a meaningful way to indicate specific behavior or to direct the compiler as to what the intention of the language is. (The compiler translates human-readable code into a form that a computer can understand.)

1. In the Project Navigator click on **Person.h** to open it.
2. Let's look at some of the code here:
   - **@interface** tells the compiler that this is the beginning of the file or beginning of the class definition.
   - **@end** tells the compiler that this is the end of the class.
3. Within those two markers, we can define properties. Property declarations have a very specific syntax, which we will work on now. Add the following bold code to define properties for name and age:

```
@interface Person : NSObject

@property NSString *name;
@property int age;

@end
```

INTRO TO iOS *Hello World: Intro to Objective-C*

- The **@property** directive tells the compiler that we want to access the attribute as a property, which means you can refer to it through dot notation. For example `person.name`
- **NSString** is an object itself. It has its own .h and .m files (found in a subfolder of the **Frameworks** folder) and can have methods and properties.
- **int** is an integer (a number value). Unlike NSString, it doesn't have methods or properties. Most of the time, when you're declaring properties, you'll probably use objects because of the added functionality.

REFERENCES

Notice the * in the declaration **NSString *name.** Whenever you're using an object as your type for a property, such as NSString (rather than a primitive, such as int), you'll likely use a * to indicate that you're declaring a reference, rather than the object itself or the value. A **Reference** holds onto the address (location) of the object. When an object is created, memory is allocated for it to store all of its values. This enables you to pass the reference between classes and into methods, so that you don't have to pass the entire object (and all its values). It's much more efficient and allows you to share objects among various programs as well as change the values in that object while it resides in one location in the memory.

PROPERTY MODIFIERS

1. We can add modifiers to any property. Add the following bold code:

   `@property `**`(strong, nonatomic)`**` NSString *name;`

   - **strong** refers to the life cycle or lifetime of the property. When an object and its properties are initially created, the app will allocate space and memory for them. When memory over the course of the app becomes scarce, the app will start to reclaim memory from objects that are no longer in use or have **weak** references to them. By specifying a strong reference here, this property will always be kept in memory for as long as the Person object is around.

   - **nonatomic** refers to how we are safeguarding access to the property. If we think there are multiple threads competing with each other, trying to change the value of the property at the same time, we want to keep the default of atomic. **atomic** locks access to the property any time the values are being changed to avoid the confusion of multiple values being set at once. The downside is that this increases the processing and makes the app slower. So if we don't think there will be conflicting values on the property, we want to specify **nonatomic.**

   - The order doesn't matter. You can use **(strong, nonatomic)** or **(nonatomic, strong).**

2A EXERCISE — Hello World: Intro to Objective-C INTRO TO iOS

2. We're also going to add a modifier for the age property. Add the following bold code:

   ```
   @property (nonatomic) int age;
   ```

   We don't need to specify strong here because memory is handled differently for primitives and it's not necessary in this instance.

   NOTE: We will be using strong and nonatomic throughout all of our exercises.

METHODS

Any time you're going to access the value of a property (either changing or reading the value), you need to use what is called a **getter** or a **setter** method (also called an **accessor** method).

1. In the Project Navigator click on **Person.m** to open it.

2. Don't add the following code, just look at it. If we were to write out the getter and setter methods for the **age** property it would look like this:

   ```
   -(int)age{
       return self.age;
   }

   -(void) setAge:(int)newAge{
       self.age = newAge;
   }
   ```

   However, Objective-C has identified this as a common programming practice and created a shortcut.

3. Add the following bold code to synthesize the properties.

   ```
   @implementation Person
   @synthesize age, name;

   @end
   ```

   This eliminates the need for us to write out the getter and setter methods. If you want to override the behavior, or do something else in those methods, or call them something different, there are ways of doing that. However, the default, and what we'll be doing throughout this entire app, is declaring a **property** in the .h file and pairing it with a **synthesize** statement in the .m file so we have our getter and setter methods ready for us.

   NOTE: In newer versions of Xcode that are being released, @synthesize is no longer required as it will be provided by default. In most cases you now only need the @property directive and Xcode takes care of synthesizing (creating getter and setter methods) for you. As you work on older projects, you'll see it was standard practice to declare a property, then add the @synthesize code, which is how this book was written. In newer versions, while @synthesize isn't necessary in most cases, using it just changes the name which you refer to properties by.

INTRO TO iOS *Hello World: Intro to Objective-C*

2A EXERCISE

ERROR ALERTS

Xcode helps you write proper code by giving hints as you type and creating error alerts when some code may be wrong or missing. While the app will run if there are yellow (warning) alerts, a red alert will prevent the app from running.

1. Around line 12, delete the **semi-colon** at the end of **@synthesize.**

2. Notice a **red error** circle ( ) appears to the left. Click on it.

3. A message will appear telling you what Xcode thinks is the problem. Double–click on **Fix-it Insert ";"** and Xcode will even fix it for you!

4. Do a **File > Save.**

5. You can't see any visual result of the work we've done so far, but you'll use this project in the next exercise. There you'll continue building a feature that you can see, so keep the file open.

METHOD SYNTAX

1. We're done making changes to the file, but let's take a closer look at the syntax of declaring and implementing a **method.** If you were actually adding a method this way, this code would be in the **.m** file above the @end line. This is just for reference, so do not add this code.

```
-(void) setAge:(int)newAge{
    self.age = newAge;
}
```

- It starts with the method type identifier, either a **dash (-)** or a **plus sign (+).** There are two kinds of methods in Objective-C: **instance methods** and **class methods.** An **instance method** is a method whose execution is scoped to a particular instance of the class. In other words, before you call an instance method, you must first create an instance of the class. Instance methods are the most common type of method. A **class method** is a method whose execution is scoped to the method's class. It does not require an instance of an object to be the receiver of a message. You often use class methods either as factory methods to create new instances of the class or to access some piece of shared information associated with the class.
- **(void)** is the return type. This method doesn't have a return type or statement, but if we wanted to return something we could return any type (primitive, object, class, etc.).
- Next is the name of the method, which in this case is **setAge.**
- After that, **(int)newAge** is a parameter for this method. A parameter is a value you are giving to the method. Methods sometimes require specific information. You send that info to it as a parameter.

Hello World: Intro to Objective-C INTRO TO iOS

- Within the **open and close curly brackets** is all the logic for the method.
- If the method is public, it needs to be declared in the .h file because the methods that are declared there are the only ones that can be seen externally.

2. If you were implementing this method, in the **.h** file you would add the following code before the @end line. (Again, this is just for reference, so do not add this code.)

```
-(void) setAge:(int)newAge;
```

This is exactly the same as the first line of the method in the .m file, only here the **open curly bracket {** is replaced with a **semi-colon ;**

INTRO TO iOS *Hello World: Finishing Up*

2B EXERCISE

EXERCISE PREVIEW

EXERCISE OVERVIEW

In this exercise, we will create a feature that allows users to input their **name** and **age**. In the previous exercise you created a **Person** class. We'll use the Person class to create an object, which will store the user's name and age. We'll then use that info to display a greeting. While Apple provides us with many classes, we must create our own classes for custom uses. Now that we've defined the class, we can use it in the View Controller.

1. If you did not complete the previous exercises (1A–2A), complete them now before starting this exercise.

2. **HelloWorld.xcodeproj** should still be open from the previous exercise. If you closed it, re-open as follows:

   – Go to **File > Open**.
   – Navigate to **Desktop > Class Files > yourname-iOS Intro Class > HelloWorld** and double–click on **HelloWorld.xcodeproj**.

SETUP

1. In the Project Navigator click on **ViewController.h**.

2B EXERCISE — Hello World: Finishing Up INTRO TO iOS

2. Under the previous **@property** statement add the following bold code and add an empty line after it to visually separate the properties from the IBAction:

   ```
   @property (strong, nonatomic) IBOutlet UILabel *theLabel;
   @property (strong, nonatomic) Person *thePerson;

   - (IBAction)sayMessage:(id)sender;
   ```

   In the above code, **Person** is the name of the class we created and **thePerson** is the name of the object we're creating. **thePerson** will be of the type **Person.**

3. In order for this view controller to use our **Person** class, it needs to know where it's defined. Add the following bold code:

   ```
   #import <UIKit/UIKit.h>
   #import "Person.h"
   ```

4. In the Project Navigator click on **ViewController.m**.

5. Add the following bold code to the synthesize line. Don't miss the comma!

   ```
   @synthesize theLabel, thePerson;
   ```

INSTANTIATION

Let's talk about creating objects from our class. We've defined our class and we've declared a property of type **Person,** but we haven't created or instantiated an object. **Instantiation** means to create an instance of a class (bringing it to life), allocating memory so that we can populate it with more values for its properties. We can think of a class as a template from which we can create many objects. For example, from our **Person** class we can create someone who has a name of John, age 40 and another person named Jenny, age 15.

In order to instantiate our Person object that we've declared as thePerson, we will go into the **viewDidLoad** method. There, we'll call **alloc** to allocate memory and **init** to initialize it. Any object that is a subclass of **NSObject** automatically has the **alloc** and **init** methods built in (this is one of the advantages of using a subclass).

1. Still in **ViewController.m** add this code shown in bold (around line 23):

   ```
       [super viewDidLoad];
       // Do any additional setup after loading the view, typically from a nib.
       theLabel.text = @"";
       thePerson = [[Person alloc] init];
   }
   ```

   NOTE: The default **init** method from NSObject is really just a placeholder that you can choose to customize with your own code.

INTRO TO iOS *Hello World: Finishing Up*

SETTING UP THE USER INTERFACE

We need to create an interface that allows the user to enter their name and age when using the app.

1. In the Project Navigator click on **Main.storyboard**.

2. At the bottom of the **Object library** ( ), search for **text field**

3. Drag two instances of **Text Field** onto the View Controller, centering them in the space above **I am going to change** so they appear as shown below.

4. Let's set some placeholder text for the text fields so the user will know what info to type inside. Click on the top **text field** to select it.

5. Go to the **Attributes inspector** ( ) on the right of the window.

6. In the field next to **Placeholder** type **Name:** and hit **Return**.

7. Click on the second **text field** to select it.

8. In the field next to **Placeholder** type **Age:** and hit **Return**.

9. We want to change the default keyboard for this field to a number keyboard. In the **Attributes inspector** ( ) next to **Keyboard** click on the menu and choose **Numbers and Punctuation.**

10. Let's make the text fields a bit wider so the user can see more of the text they enter. Select the **Name:** text field and go into the **Size inspector** tab ( ).

11. Change the Width to **200** and hit **Return**.

12. Repeat the previous step for the **Age:** text field.

13. Let's add another button. In the **Object library** ( ) search for **button**

14. Drag out a **Button** and center it below the Age text field.

15. With the button selected, switch to the **Attributes inspector** tab ( ).

NOBLE DESKTOP — STEP BY STEP TRAINING — NOBLEDESKTOP.COM

Hello World: Finishing Up   INTRO TO iOS

16. Scroll down to the View options and set **Background** to **Light Gray Color.**

17. Under the Button options further up, set the following:

    Text Color: **White Color**
    Inset, Top and Bottom: **8**
    Inset, Left and Right: **15**

18. Double–click on the Button, type **Set Person Info** and hit **Return.**

    NOTE: This app now has two buttons. One button will change the person's info (by storing the information in an object in the app's memory) and a second button that will change the label on screen (so you can see that it successfully pulled that info from memory). In real life you'd probably do this with a single button, but we're intentionally using two buttons because we want it to be clear that one deals with the object and the other deals with the label.

19. Re-center the button by moving it to the left, until the blue guides show up.

20. If the Document Outline is open, click **Hide Document Outline** (▢).

21. At the top right of the window, click on the **Assistant editor** button (▢). **ViewController.h** should be shown on the right.

SETTING UP OUTLETS

1. We need to be able to address the text fields programmatically, so let's create outlets for them. Hold **Ctrl** and drag from the **Name text field** in the Editor, into the code as shown. (Drag to below the second @property.)

2. In the menu that pops up, set:
   – Connection: **Outlet**
   – Name: **nameTextField**
   – Type: **UITextField**
   – Storage: **Strong**

3. Click **Connect.**

INTRO TO iOS *Hello World: Finishing Up*

4. Now let's do the same for the Age. Hold **Ctrl** and drag from the **Age text field** into the code below the last @property.

5. In the menu that pops up, set:
   - Connection: **Outlet**
   - Name: **ageTextField**
   - Type: **UITextField**
   - Storage: **Strong**

6. Click **Connect**.

7. We have to do this one more time for the button, but because buttons are associated with methods, we'll put it below the other method. Hold **Ctrl** and drag from the **Set Person Info** button into the code below - **(IBAction)**.

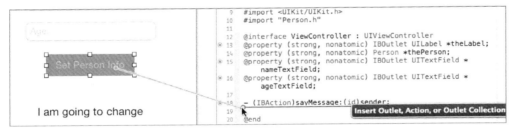

8. In the menu that pops up, set:
   - Connection: **Action**
   - Name: **setPersonInfo**
   - Type: **id**
   - Event: **Touch Up Inside**
   - Arguments: **Sender**

9. Click **Connect**.

10. At the top right of the window, click on the **Standard editor** button (📄).

11. In the Project Navigator click on **ViewController.m**.

12. Let's not forget to synthesize the properties we just created. Add the following bold code to the synthesize code (around line 16):

    `@synthesize theLabel, thePerson,` **`nameTextField, ageTextField`**`;`

2B EXERCISE — Hello World: Finishing Up — INTRO TO iOS

DOT NOTATION VS. GETTER AND SETTER METHODS

1. Still in **ViewController.m,** find the **setPersonInfo** method near the bottom (around line 42).

2. Here we want to take the values that were entered into each text field and set them onto the corresponding properties on our Person object. We can do this through **dot notation.** Add the following bold code:

```
- (IBAction)setPersonInfo:(id)sender {
    thePerson.name = nameTextField.text;
    thePerson.age = ageTextField.text;
}
```

> **SYNTAXES**
>
> Alternatively, we could have used the **getter** and **setter methods** instead of dot notation. We'll show you this code so you know how it would look, but don't add it to your code:
>
> ```
> - (IBAction)setPersonInfo:(id)sender {
>     [thePerson setName:nameTextField.text];
>     [thePerson setAge:ageTextField.text];
> }
> ```
>
> If you look at these two sets of commands (the code you added and the code above), they're almost identical. The first one is using dot notation to set the name and age value and the second is using method calls. Either one can be used for properties. However, the second is the appropriate one to use for simple method calls that aren't property getters or setters (also called accessors).

3. We also want some visual confirmation that these values have been set. Add the following bold code:

```
- (IBAction)setPersonInfo:(id)sender {
    thePerson.name = nameTextField.text;
    thePerson.age = ageTextField.text;
    theLabel.text = @"Ready to Display Text";
}
```

PLACEHOLDERS FOR VALUES

Now we want to create a setup for after the user's info has been set onto the Person object. If the user taps on the **Display the Text** button, we want it to display something like **Hello Steve age 56.**

1. In order to do this, around line 34, delete the if else statement so the code looks like this:

```
- (IBAction)sayMessage:(id)sender {

}
```

PAGE 50 — INTRO TO iPHONE/iPAD APP DEVELOPMENT

INTRO TO iOS *Hello World: Finishing Up*

2B EXERCISE

2. Add the following bold code.

   ```
   - (IBAction)sayMessage:(id)sender {
       theLabel.text = [NSString stringWithFormat:@"Hello %@ age %d"];
   }
   ```

   We're going to be displaying **Hello, name** and the **age**. We're using a method on the **NSString** object called **stringWithFormat:**. This allows us to type in placeholders and fill them in with specific object values. In this case, **%@** references a string that will be substituted in for this symbol. **%d** substitutes for a decimal or number. Now we need to specify what values we want to have substituted in.

3. Add the following bold code. Don't miss the comma after `@"Hello %@ age %d"`

   ```
   - (IBAction)sayMessage:(id)sender {
       theLabel.text = [NSString stringWithFormat:@"Hello %@ age %d", thePerson.name, thePerson.age];
   }
   ```

   NOTE: **thePerson.name** and **thePerson.age** will be substituted in for **%@** and **%d**.

4. Let's test this out to see how it looks. At the top left of the window click the **Run** button (▶).

5. After iOS Simulator loads, click into the **Name text field** and type your name.

6. Then click into the **Age text field** and type your age.

7. Click the **Set Person Info** button.

   Notice there are two problems: the keyboard is not going away and the text field that is supposed to say "Ready to Display Text" isn't fully showing.

8. Click the **return** key and notice it doesn't dismiss the keyboard either!

9. Let's fix the text field problem now. Switch back to Xcode.

10. In the Project Navigator, switch over to **Main.storyboard.**

11. Select any element on the page (like one of the buttons) and go to **Editor > Resolve Auto Layout Issues > Reset to Suggested Constraints.**

12. In the top-left corner of the toolbar, click on the **Run** (▶) button **(Cmd–R).**

    NOTE: If you get a warning asking if you want to **Stop "HelloWorld"**, click **Stop.**

13. Type in your name and age, then click the **Set Person Info** button. Notice the full text for the label is now showing, which means that the values on the Person object have been set. Awesome!

14. It's time to fix the problem with the keyboard not dismissing. Switch back to Xcode.

    In Xcode if you notice a yellow alert message in the code, just ignore that for now, we'll fix that later.

NOBLE DESKTOP — STEP BY STEP TRAINING — NOBLEDESKTOP.COM

Hello World: Finishing Up INTRO TO iOS

FIRST RESPONDER, DELEGATES AND DISMISSING THE KEYBOARD

When a text field is tapped into, it gains the status of **first responder,** meaning that any keyboard events will go into that text field. The app needs to know who the first responder is for events. In order to change this, either another controller must become first responder or the current controller must resign first responder status. This doesn't happen automatically, so we need to add this to the code.

We need to intercept a method, which gets called when the **return** key is tapped, and tell the control that it's resigning as first responder. In order to do that, we need to assign delegates of **self** to both the name and age text fields (**self** sets it to the class or object it's currently in).

1. In the Project Navigator, click on **ViewController.m.**

2. In `viewDidLoad` (which starts around line 18) add the following bold code:

    ```
    thePerson = [[Person alloc] init];
    nameTextField.delegate = self;
    ageTextField.delegate = self;
    }
    ```

    These text fields will both delegate specific behavior to methods within the ViewController class. In order for this view controller to become a delegate for a text field, it needs to declare itself as such in the class definition.

3. In the Project Navigator click on **ViewController.h.**

4. We need to indicate that UIViewController can also be a delegate for a UITextField by adding the following bold code (around line 12):

    ```
    @interface ViewController : UIViewController<UITextFieldDelegate>
    ```

    The code is stating that this class is conforming to a protocol of **UITextFieldDelegate.** A **delegate** is a protocol that defines a set of methods that a class can implement. UITextFieldDelegate is interesting because all of the methods in it are optional. UITextFieldDelegate is provided so that the programmer can have a little bit more control over the text field and intercept events before anything happens. Let's take a look at the UITextFieldDelegate in Xcode Help to find the method associated with the return key event.

5. Go to **Help > Documentation and API Reference.**

6. Into the search field type **UITextFieldDelegate** and wait a moment for results.

7. Click on the first result (which should be for **UITextFieldDelegate**).

8. Scroll down to the **Tasks** section.

    As you can see there aren't many methods. The pattern here is that these are all methods that are intercepting behavior before or after something occurs. It gives the programmer a little bit more control. The one we are going to use is textFieldShouldReturn:.

PAGE 52   INTRO TO iPHONE/iPAD APP DEVELOPMENT

INTRO TO iOS *Hello World: Finishing Up*

2B EXERCISE

9. Click on **textFieldShouldReturn:**.

   This asks the delegate if the text field should process the pressing of the return button. We need to return a Yes if the text field should implement its default behavior for the return button. It's important to note that the text field calls this method whenever the user taps the return button. We can use this method to implement any custom behavior when the button is tapped. We now know that when the return button is hit the app is going to jump into this method.

10. Copy the line of code for the **textFieldShouldReturn:** method:

    ```
    - (BOOL)textFieldShouldReturn:(UITextField *)textField
    ```

11. Close the Documentation window.

12. In the Project Navigator click on **ViewController.m**.

13. Paste the code above the **@end** line at the bottom of all the code:

    ```
    - (BOOL)textFieldShouldReturn:(UITextField *)textField

    @end
    ```

14. Add an open and close bracket at the end of the line of code you just pasted:

    ```
    - (BOOL)textFieldShouldReturn:(UITextField *)textField{

    }

    @end
    ```

15. When the return button is tapped we want to dismiss the keyboard. The way to do that is by calling resignFirstResponder on the text field. Basically when a user taps into the text field, it is considered the first responder to user events and has control. In order to relinquish that control and allow other controls and views to interact with the user, we need to call this resignFirstResponder method.

    Add the following bold code to the **textFieldShouldReturn:** method:

    ```
    - (BOOL)textFieldShouldReturn:(UITextField *)textField{
        [textField resignFirstResponder];
    }
    ```

16. This method also needs a return value of YES or NO. To say we are accepting the event of the user tapping return, add the following bold code:

    ```
    - (BOOL)textFieldShouldReturn:(UITextField *)textField{
        [textField resignFirstResponder];
        return YES;
    }
    ```

17. Let's see how that changes things. Click the **Run** button (▶).

    NOTE: If you get a warning asking if you want to **Stop "HelloWorld"**, click **Stop**.

18. After the iOS Simulator loads, add your **name** and **age** again and then hit **return**. This should dismiss the keyboard.

Hello World: Finishing Up INTRO TO iOS

19. Leave the app running in the iOS Simulator. We'll come back to it in a moment.

20. Switch back to Xcode (you should still be in **ViewController.m**).

THE DEBUGGER AREA AND BREAKPOINTS

As you program your app, there are times you'll want to see what's happening in the code at a specific point without waiting until it's been programmed to show up on screen. You can easily do this by creating Breakpoints.

A **Breakpoint** stops execution at that line and does not continue. You can create a Breakpoint by clicking in the gutter to the left of any line of code. It will be indicated by a blue arrow.

1. Around line 39 you should find `thePerson.name = nameTextField.text;`

2. Click on the line number for that line to create a **Breakpoint:**

   ```
   38    - (IBAction)setPersonInfo:(id)sender {
   39          thePerson.name = nameTextField.text;
   40          thePerson.age = ageTextField.text;
   41          theLabel.text = @"Ready to Display Text";
   42    }
   ```

3. Click the **Run** button (▶).

   NOTE: If you get a warning asking if you want to **Stop "HelloWorld"**, click **Stop**.

4. Set your name and age, then click the **Set Person Info** button.

5. You should be taken back to Xcode, and the **Debugger** area should have opened at the bottom. There you will find controls to help you step through the execution of the app more slowly. For example, we've just stepped into **setPersonInfo.** We're about to change the name to what was entered in the text field. As shown to the right, click the **arrow** to the left of **thePerson** to expand its values.

6. Notice that up to the Breakpoint, thePerson object exists but the values have not yet been set to the info you entered (instead the age is **0** and the age is **nil** or nothing).

7. Click on the **Step over** button ( ). Look at the **Debugger** area and see that the **name** now has your name in it!

8. Click the **Step over** button ( ) again. This should have changed the age value to your age, however, there is a bug in the code, as we can see in the Debugger.

   The reason we're seeing a long number rather than your age is because the current code is trying to assign a text string to an integer. Remember to be careful when using different data types, especially going between numbers and strings, to know what type you want.

   The good thing is, there's an easy fix for this. You should already be looking at the **ViewController.m** code (above the Debugger area).

INTRO TO iOS *Hello World: Finishing Up*

9. There's a method called **intValue** that will convert the string to an int for us. We'll also add **brackets** to convert the line from a dot notation to a method call. Edit line 40 like so:

   ```
   thePerson.age = [ageTextField.text intValue];
   ```

10. Do a **File > Save**.

11. Time for another test. Click the **Run** button (▶).

    NOTE: If you get a warning asking if you want to **Stop "HelloWorld"**, click **Stop**.

12. After the iOS Simulator loads, add your **name** and **age** again and then hit **return**.

13. Click the **Set Person Info** button.

14. This should take you back to Xcode. In the **Debugger** area, click **Step over** ( ) twice.

15. Now the Debugger should be showing both the correct age and name.

16. At this point, we no longer need the Breakpoint. **Delete** it by dragging the **Breakpoint** off the line number (to the left or right). It should disappear in a poof!

17. In the Debugger, click the **Continue program execution** button ( ).

18. You should be switched back to the iOS Simulator.

19. Click the **Display the Text** button. Check out the app saying hello to you!

20. Try inputting a different name and age.

21. Hit **return** to close the keyboard.

22. Click the **Set Person Info** button to set the info on the Person object.

23. Click the **Display the Text** button to actually display the new values.

24. Switch back to Xcode.

25. Click the **Stop** button ( ).

26. That's all for this beginner app, so you can close this Xcode project.

    There's a lot more to learn, but hopefully you're starting to get a better understanding of Objective-C and programming for iOS.

INTRO TO iOS *Creating Simple Cells & Managing Retina Images*

EXERCISE PREVIEW

EXERCISE OVERVIEW

In the next series of exercises we'll build an app for the Jive Factory, a music venue. In this exercise, we'll get started by mocking up a list of upcoming shows. You will also learn how to deal with images for Apple's high-resolution Retina devices.

SETUP

1. In Xcode, go to **File > New > Project** to create a new project.

2. In the categories on the left, under **iOS** make sure **Application** is selected.

3. On the right side, double–click on the **Single View Application** template.

4. Set the following:
   – Product Name: **Jive Factory**
   – Organization Name: **Noble Desktop**
   – Company Identifier: **com.nobledesktop**
   – Class Prefix: (leave blank)
   – Devices: **iPhone**

5. Click **Next**.

6. Navigate to **Desktop > Class Files > yourname-iOS Intro Class**.

7. Check **Create git repository on My Mac** if it is not already checked.

8. Click **Create**.

2C Creating Simple Cells & Managing Retina Images INTRO TO iOS
EXERCISE

9. In the Project Navigator, in the **Jive Factory** folder, notice that a few files were created automatically. Because we chose Single View Application when creating this project, Xcode automatically created a View Controller linked to a header file (ViewController.h) and an implementation file (ViewController.m) as well as AppDelegate.h and AppDelegate.m files.

ADDING CELLS

1. Click on **Main.storyboard**.

2. Make sure the **Document Outline** is showing. If you don't see it, click the **Show Document Outline** button (▶) at the bottom left of the Editor area.

3. In the **Document Outline,** expand **View Controller Scene** then click on **View Controller** to select it.

   We want more functionality than what the default View Controller provides. Let's replace it with a Table View Controller.

4. With the **View Controller** still selected, hit **Delete.**

5. At the bottom right of the window, in the **Object library** (▣), find the **Table View Controller** object.

6. Drag the **Table View Controller** onto the Editor.

7. In the **Document Outline,** expand **Table View Controller** if it is not already expanded.

8. Click on **Table View.**

9. In the **Utilities** area on the right, click on the **Attributes inspector** tab (▤).

10. Under **Table View,** from the **Content** menu, choose **Static Cells.**

    NOTE: In a later exercise we'll show you how to create Dynamic Prototype cells using code. In this exercise, we just want to mockup what this View Controller will look like, so we'll use Static Cells for now.

11. In the **Document Outline,** expand **Table View.**

12. Expand **Table View Section.**

13. Notice there are three Table View Cells listed. Right now we only want to work with one, which we'll make copies of later so let's delete the two extra Table View Cells. Click on the **second** Table View Cell to select it.

14. Hold **Shift** and click on the **last** Table View Cell to select them both.

15. Hit **Delete.**

16. Click the remaining **Table View Cell** to select it.

17. In the **Attributes inspector** (▤) on the right, set the **Style** menu to **Subtitle.**

PAGE 58 INTRO TO iPHONE/iPAD APP DEVELOPMENT

INTRO TO iOS *Creating Simple Cells & Managing Retina Images*

EXERCISE

18. In the **Document Outline,** expand **Table View Cell** then expand **Content View.**

19. Notice there are two labels: **Title** and **Subtitle.** Click on **Label - Title.**

20. In the **Attributes inspector** ( ), below the Text menu in the field that currently says Title, delete the text and change it to:
    Nicole Atkins

    NOTE: Xcode is finicky sometimes, so you will not be able to see the entire text now. We will fix it soon—the text will fully display once we add an image.

21. Click on **Label - Subtitle.**

22. Underneath the Text menu in the field that currently says Subtitle, change it to:
    Tue 5/1

ADDING IMAGES

We want to add an image of the band to the cell. First we need to add the images we will be using to our project.

1. Go to **File > Add Files to "Jive Factory".**

2. Navigate to the **Desktop,** then go to **Class Files > yourname-iOS Intro Class > Band Images > thumbnails > regular.**

3. Press **Cmd–A** to select all the images in that folder.

4. At the bottom of the window, set the following:

    Destination: Check **Copy items into destination group's folder (if needed)**
    Folders: No folders are being added, so leave as is.
    Add to targets: Check on **Jive Factory.**

5. Click the **Add** button.

6. In the Project Navigator, notice the files have been added to our Jive Factory folder. To keep things organized, let's move these to the **Supporting Files** folder.

7. In the Project Navigator click on **thumb-ambulance-ltd.png** (or whichever photo is listed first) to select it.

8. **Shift–click** on **thumb-sleepies.png** (or the last image) to select all the images.

9. Drag them into the **Supporting Files** folder.

10. Click on **Main.storyboard.**

11. Now we'll add the image to the Table View Cell. In the **Document Outline,** click on **Table View Cell.**

NOBLE DESKTOP — STEP BY STEP TRAINING — NOBLEDESKTOP.COM

Creating Simple Cells & Managing Retina Images INTRO TO iOS

12. In the **Attributes inspector** ( ) on the right, from the **Image** menu, choose **thumb-nicole-atkins.png** as shown below. If you don't see the option, click on **Main.storyboard** to make sure it's selected.

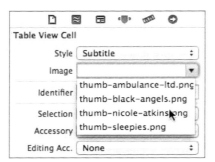

13. In the **Editor,** notice the thumbnail image has been added next to the title. It's a little smaller than it should be. Right now it's being resized because the cell isn't tall enough. Let's make the cell taller.

14. In the **Utilities** area on the right, click the **Size inspector** tab ( ).

15. Next to **Row Height**, enter **88** and press **Return.**

16. In the **Editor,** notice the improved look of our cell. Awesome!

ADDING MORE CELLS

1. In the **Document Outline**, click on **Table View Section.**

2. In the **Utilities** area on the right, click the **Attributes inspector** tab ( ).

3. Next to **Rows** change 1 to **3** and hit **Return.** Voilà! We now have three copies of the original cell in the Editor!

4. In the Editor, click on the **second** Nicole Atkins cell.

5. In the **Attributes inspector** ( ), from the **Image** menu, choose **thumb-ambulance-ltd.png**

6. In the **Editor,** notice the image changed in the second cell.

7. Double–click the **Nicole Atkins** text in the second cell and change it to:
Ambulance LTD

8. Double–click the **Tue 5/1** text below that and change it to:
Fri 5/4

9. In the **Editor,** click on the **last** Nicole Atkins cell.

10. In the **Attributes inspector** ( ), from the **Image** menu choose **thumb-sleepies.png**

11. Double–click the **Nicole Atkins** text in the third cell and change it to:
Sleepies

PAGE 60 INTRO TO iPHONE/iPAD APP DEVELOPMENT

INTRO TO IOS *Creating Simple Cells & Managing Retina Images*

12. Double–click the **Tue 5/1** text below that and change it to:
    Sat 5/5

13. Let's preview our work so far. Make sure the active **Scheme** (top-left corner) is set to **Jive Factory > iPhone Retina (4-inch)**.

14. Click the **Run** button (▶). The iOS Simulator may take a while to load. After it loads, you won't be able to do anything in the app, but you can see the layout.

15. The layout is displaying, but notice that the lines that separate the cells do not extend all the way across the screen. To fix that, go back to Xcode (keep the app running and the simulator open so you can use it once we fix the lines).

16. In the Document Outline, select **Table View.**

17. In the **Attributes inspector** ( ) from the **Separator Insets** menu click **Custom.**

18. Set both Left and Right to **0**.

ADDING RETINA IMAGES

1. Switch back to the **iOS Simulator.**

   Notice the images appear pixelated at the Retina resolution. Retina displays are twice the resolution of regular displays. Therefore, an image that is 30x30 on a regular screen will display as 60x60 on a Retina screen. Because of this higher pixel density, to provide crisp images for these devices we also have to include higher-resolution images in the app.

2. Switch back to **Xcode.**

3. Go to **File > Add Files to "Jive Factory"**.

4. Navigate to the **Desktop**, then go to **Class Files > yourname-iOS Intro Class > Band Images > thumbnails > retina.**

5. Press **Cmd–A** to select all the images in that folder.

6. At the bottom of the window, set the following:

   Destination: Check **Copy items into destination group's folder (if needed)**
   Folders: No folders are being added, so leave as is.
   Add to targets: Check on **Jive Factory.**

7. Click **Add.**

8. In the Project Navigator, the files have been added to the **Jive Factory** folder. Notice that we gave them the same name as the regular images, but added **@2x** at the end. This important naming convention allows apps to automatically detect the higher-resolution images and display them instead of the regular images. So keep in mind that you'll need to make two sets of graphics, with the @2x being twice the pixel dimensions of the smaller version. If you start designing Retina graphics, be sure that you can divide their size evenly in half!

Creating Simple Cells & Managing Retina Images INTRO TO iOS

9. To keep things organized, let's move these to the **Supporting Files** folder. In the Project Navigator click on **thumb-ambulance-ltd@2x.png** (or the whichever image is listed first) to select it.

10. **Shift–click** on **thumb-sleepies@2x.png** (or the last photo) to select all the images.

11. Drag them into the **Supporting Files** folder.

    That's all you have to do. The app will automatically choose the higher-resolution images because of the @2x naming convention!

12. Click the **Run** button (▶).

    NOTE: If you get a warning asking if you want to **Stop "Jive Factory"**, click **Stop**.

13. When the app finishes loading on the iOS Simulator, notice the separators between cells extend fully across the screen. Our images also appear crisp and are no longer pixelated. Sweet!

    NOTE: The first cell is partially beneath the translucent status bar at the top. We'll fix this issue soon. For now this is OK.

14. Switch back to Xcode.

15. Click the **Stop** button (■).

16. In the Project Navigator click on **Main.storyboard**.

17. Go to **File > Save**.

18. Leave the project open. We'll continue building this app in the next exercise.

MORE INFO ABOUT IMAGES

For all images and icons, Apple recommends PNG 24 (called PNG 32 in Adobe Fireworks). It supports alpha-transparency and doesn't lose quality. Avoid using interlaced PNGs. Keep in mind that the background color of some parts of the UI aren't pure white (such as in the table rows). So if you want your images to use transparency effects, it is best to take advantage of PNG's alpha-transparency by creating your images on a transparent background instead of on a white background.

Remember that when you are creating images, it is best to start with the highest quality image or a vector image and then scale down to the size you want to use. When you've scaled it, then you can clean up the image by removing excess details, if needed.

INTRO TO iOS

Section Topics
SECTION 3

BUILDING A TABLE VIEW CONTROLLER
Creating a Class and Connecting it to the Storyboard
Adding Properties for the Band Data
Editing the Three DataSource Protocol Methods

THE NAVIGATION CONTROLLER
Navigation Controllers
Setting the Initial View Controller
Setting the Root View Controller
Adding the Detail View Controller
Segues

CREATING THE BAND DETAIL VIEW
Adding Label Objects
Adding View Objects
Changing Text Properties
Adding a Divider Line
Adding the Band Images

INTRO TO IOS *Building a Table View Controller*

3A EXERCISE

EXERCISE PREVIEW

EXERCISE OVERVIEW

The list of upcoming shows we built in the previous exercise is looking good, but we really need these cells to be created dynamically so they are easier to update when we need to add more shows. In this exercise, we will dynamically populate the table using code, instead of manually setting each cell in the Editor.

1. If you did not complete the previous exercise (2C), complete it now before starting this exercise.

2. **Jive Factory.xcodeproj** should still be open from the previous exercise. If you closed it, re-open as follows:

   – Go to **File > Open**.
   – Navigate to **Desktop > Class Files > yourname-iOS Intro Class > Jive Factory** and double–click on **Jive Factory.xcodeproj**.

GETTING STARTED

We want to keep the look and feel of the cells we built in the previous exercise. We'll use the first cell as a template, but we don't need the rest of them.

1. In the **Editor**, click the **Ambulance LTD** cell to select it.

2. **Shift–click** on the **Sleepies** cell to select them both.

3. Hit **Delete**.

4. In the **Document Outline**, click **Table View** to select it.

5. In the **Attributes inspector** ( ), from the **Content** menu choose **Dynamic Prototypes**.

NOBLE DESKTOP — STEP BY STEP TRAINING — NOBLEDESKTOP.COM   PAGE 65

3A EXERCISE
Building a Table View Controller — INTRO TO iOS

6. In the **Document Outline**, select **Table View Cell**.

7. In the **Attributes inspector** ( ), next to **Identifier** type **bandCell** and hit **Return**. This defines a name we can use to programmatically refer to this later.

CREATING A CLASS

We need to create a new class that we can customize to populate the cells dynamically.

1. In the Project Navigator, select **ViewController.m**. (We want the file to be added after this file, that's why we had you select it.)

2. Go to **File > New > File**.

3. Double-click **Objective-C class** to choose it.

4. From the **Subclass of** menu, choose **UITableViewController**. (Be careful to choose the UI**Table**ViewController, not the UIViewController!)

5. Edit the name of the **Class** to be **BandsTableViewController**

   NOTE: UITableViewController is the object we are currently using on the storyboard. By making our class a subclass of the UITableViewController, it will have all the functionality it currently has, plus any additional functionality we add in the code to this new BandsTableViewController class.

6. Click **Next**.

7. You should already be in the **Jive Factory** folder, so click **Create**.

8. Notice **BandsTableViewController.h** and **BandsTableViewController.m** have been added in the Project Navigator. Now we have a class we can work with.

CONNECTING THE CLASS TO THE STORYBOARD

Now we need to connect our Table View Controller to the class we just created.

1. In the Project Navigator, click on **Main.storyboard**.

2. In the **Document Outline**, click **Table View**.

3. In the **Utilities** area on the right, click on the **Connections inspector** tab ( ).

4. Notice there are two outlets that are assigned to the Table View: **dataSource** and **delegate**.

INTRO TO IOS *Building a Table View Controller*

3A
EXERCISE

The dataSource and delegate are two protocols that need to be defined in order to populate a Table View. Protocols are agreements between one class and another that a class is going to conform to or implement certain methods. For example, the dataSource protocol defines methods that will provide data to our table view. When you create a table view controller by dragging it from the Object library as we did in the previous exercise, it defaults to itself being the dataSource and delegate for the table view. Once we connect our new class to this view, the new class will be used at the dataSource and delegate and therefore we can control the flow of data to the table view.

5. Let's connect the view we have in the storyboard to our new class. In the **Document Outline**, click **Table View Controller**.

6. In the **Utilities** area on the right, click the **Identity inspector** tab ( ).

7. Next to **Class**, type **B** and Xcode should autocomplete to **BandsTableViewController**

    NOTE: Sometimes Xcode takes a while to recognize a new class, so if you do not see any autocomplete suggestions, you will just have to type it in manually.

8. Hit **Return** to apply the change.

9. In the **Document Outline**, click **Table View**.

10. In the **Utilities** area on the right, click the **Connections inspector** tab ( ).

11. Notice that **dataSource** and **delegate** are now connected to the Bands Table View Controller. Awesome! Now we can start adding the code we need to populate the cells.

ADDING PROPERTIES FOR THE BAND DATA

Before we can draw the table and all the cells, we need to represent the data (title, subtitle, images) for all the bands in the code as well. Let's start by creating properties for the Title, Subtitle, and Image in the header file.

1. In the Project Navigator, click on **BandsTableViewController.h** to open it.

2. Add the following property for the band title around line 12:

    ```
    @interface BandsTableViewController : UITableViewController
    @property (strong, nonatomic) NSArray *bandTitles;
    ```

    This creates a property called **bandTitles** of the type NSArray. Arrays are one of the most common and powerful types of variables. Simply put, an array holds lots of information that is grouped together. Think of it as a list. The items in the array can be accessed by their number, starting with 0 for the first item in the array.

Building a Table View Controller INTRO TO iOS

3. Let's create the rest of the properties. After the bandTitles property, add the following code:

```
@property (strong, nonatomic) NSArray *bandTitles;
@property (strong, nonatomic) NSArray *bandSubtitles;
@property (strong, nonatomic) NSArray *bandImageNames;

@end
```

4. Next let's synthesize these properties in the implementation file to make them available for use. In the Project Navigator click on **BandsTableViewController.m**.

5. If you don't see line numbers next to the code, go into **Xcode > Preferences** and:
   – Click on the **Text Editing** tab.
   – Check on **Line numbers** (which is in the **Editing** subtab).
   – Close the **Preferences** window.

6. After the implementation code (around line 15), add the following **bold** code to synthesize the properties we added in the header file:

```
@implementation BandsTableViewController

@synthesize bandTitles;
@synthesize bandSubtitles;
@synthesize bandImageNames;

- (id)initWithStyle:(UITableViewStyle)style
```

7. Now we need to define these arrays with the info for the bands. To save you some time, we've already written the code for these arrays for you. Go to **File > Open**.

8. Navigate to **Class Files > yourname-iOS Intro Class > Code Snippets** and open **band-arrays.txt**.

9. Press **Cmd–A** to select all the code.

10. Press **Cmd–C** to copy it.

11. Close the file.

    You should still have **BandsTableViewController.m** open.

12. Find the **viewDidLoad** method (around line 30).

13. Select the four lines of green comment code:

```
// Uncomment the following line to preserve selection between presentations.
// self.clearsSelectionOnViewWillAppear = NO;

// Uncomment the following line to display an Edit button in the navigation bar for this view controller.
// self.navigationItem.rightBarButtonItem = self.editButtonItem;
```

INTRO TO IOS *Building a Table View Controller*

14. Press **Cmd–V** to paste the code, replacing the comments with the array. You should end up with the code as follows:

```
- (void)viewDidLoad
{
    [super viewDidLoad];

    bandTitles = [[NSArray alloc] initWithObjects:@"Nicole Atkins", @"Ambulance LTD",
@"Sleepies", @"Black Angels",nil];

    bandSubtitles = [[NSArray alloc] initWithObjects:@"Tue 5/1", @"Fri 5/4", @"Sat 5/5", @"Sun
5/6",nil];

    bandImageNames = [[NSArray alloc] initWithObjects:@"thumb-nicole-atkins.png", @"thumb-
ambulance-ltd.png", @"thumb-sleepies.png", @"thumb-black-angels.png",nil];

}

- (void)didReceiveMemoryWarning
```

Let's break this code down for you. We are setting each of the properties we created earlier (bandTitles, bandSubtitles, and bandImageNames) to a new NSArray object. The object is being created by allocating memory to it. It is being initialized with some data. The data is a list of strings (shown in red in Xcode). Each value is separated by a comma. The list ends with a nil variable to signify the end of the array. As we mentioned earlier, the data in an array can be accessed by a number. For example, the first item in bandTitles (Nicole Atkins) is equal to 0. The second value (Ambulance LTD) is equal to 1 and so on.

15. Go to **File > Save**.

EDITING THE THREE DATASOURCE PROTOCOL METHODS

When we created the **BandsTableViewController** class, Xcode automatically provided us with methods to use. Some of the methods are optional and have been commented out. Others have commented code before them, which are hints that Xcode gives us for methods that we might want to implement to customize the look, feel and data that we want in our app.

1. Around line 47, find the **#pragma mark - Table view data source** comment code.

2. Below that, there are three methods we'll need to modify to get the band information displaying in our app:

- **numberOfSectionsInTableView:** (around line 49)
- **numberOfRowsInSection:** (around line 56)
- **cellForRowAtIndexPath:** (around line 63)

Building a Table View Controller INTRO TO iOS

3. These methods are part of the dataSource protocol. The first method is **numberOfSectionsInTableView:**. This method returns the number of sections so that the BandsTableViewController knows how many to draw and how many to loop through. We'll just have one section, so change **0** to **1** as shown below:

```
- (NSInteger)numberOfSectionsInTableView:(UITableView *)tableView
{
#warning Potentially incomplete method implementation.
    // Return the number of sections.
    return 1;
}
```

4. The next method is **numberOfRowsInSection:**. This method will be called for each section in the table. Since we only have one section, it will only be called once. We need to return the total number of bands that will be drawn. This number will depend on the number of bands we have, which varies but we can get the number of bands by accessing the size of our array with some simple code. Add the following bold code to the **numberOfRowsInSection:** method, replacing the **0**:

```
- (NSInteger)tableView:(UITableView *)tableView numberOfRowsInSection:(NSInteger)section
{
#warning Incomplete method implementation.
    // Return the number of rows in the section.
    return [bandTitles count];
}
```

This code takes the array **bandTitles** and accesses a method called **count**. The count method gives us the size of the array. Now that this method has the size of the array, it tells the View Controller how many times to call the next method, **cellForRowAtIndexPath:**.

cellForRowAtIndexPath: returns the cell object with all the data it needs to draw the title, subtitle, and image. This is called for each row and it passes in a parameter called **indexPath,** which will tell us which row is currently being called for. What we need to do is build a cell object with the data we want the table to draw.

5. Let's take a look at the code in this method. Find the following line of code (around line 65):

```
static NSString *CellIdentifier = @"Cell";
```

6. If you remember, earlier in the exercise we set the Cell Identifier of the Nicole Atkins cell in the storyboard to **bandCell.** To target the cell on our storyboard we need to edit this code.

7. As shown below, change **Cell** to **bandCell**

```
static NSString *CellIdentifier = @"bandCell";
```

INTRO TO IOS *Building a Table View Controller*

Now that we have the correct cell being targeted let's look at the rest of the code. The code in cellForRowAtIndexPath: grabs the cell from the storyboard by using a method **dequeueReusableCellWithIdentifier:** to pass in the Identifier cell. The method is called and passes in an **indexPath** variable to the tableView object. **indexPath** specifies the section and row that it will be working with. That instantiates a cell object, which we want to further customize by adding our band data into it.

8. Find the **// Configure the cell** comment code around line 68.

9. This is where we will be adding the code that will customize the cells with our band info. Let's start with the Title. We need to access the label for the Title in our cell. The title label is represented by the attribute **textLabel**. We need to redefine the **text** in the **textLabel** in the **cell**. Add the following bold code:

   ```
   // Configure the cell...
   cell.textLabel.text = [];
   return cell;
   ```

   This will target the cell's textLabel's text (the Title) and change it to what we put in the brackets. We want to set it to the info in our array.

10. Add the following bold code:

    ```
    // Configure the cell...
    cell.textLabel.text = [bandTitles objectAtIndex:indexPath.row];
    return cell;
    ```

    bandTitles is the name of the array with the Title info.
    objectAtIndex:indexPath.row gets the info from the array at a specific value. That value is the row that is currently being populated.

11. Let's see our code in action. Click the **Run** button (▶).

    NOTE: If you get a warning asking if you want to **Stop "Jive Factory"**, click **Stop**.

12. When the app finishes loading, it will open in the iOS Simulator. Notice we have four cells, each with the different band title. You may also notice the cells are shorter than in the previous exercise. That's because we're now doing things programmatically. We'll fix that later in this exercise.

    NOTE: The translucent status bar partially covers up some of the text and the image, obscuring part of the content. We will fix this issue in the next exercise.

13. We still need to set the show date and band image. Switch back to Xcode.

14. The code for the **subtitle** is similar to the Title but it uses an attribute called **detailTextLabel** instead of textLabel. Add the following bold code:

    ```
    // Configure the cell...
    cell.textLabel.text = [bandTitles objectAtIndex:indexPath.row];
    cell.detailTextLabel.text = [];
    return cell;
    ```

Building a Table View Controller — INTRO TO iOS

15. Set the detailTextLabel to use the bandSubtitles array and get the info from it by adding the following bold code:

    ```
    // Configure the cell...
    cell.textLabel.text = [bandTitles objectAtIndex:indexPath.row];
    cell.detailTextLabel.text = [bandSubtitles objectAtIndex:indexPath.row];
    return cell;
    ```

16. Click the **Run** button (▶).

    NOTE: If you get a warning asking if you want to Stop "Jive Factory", click **Stop**.

    When the app finishes loading, it will open in the iOS Simulator. Now the dates should all be different as well. All that's left are the images.

17. Switch back to Xcode.

18. Click the **Stop** button (■).

19. The code for adding images is a bit more complicated because we only have the names of the images stored, not the actual objects. We'll need to use a method that will find the file, create an image and assign it to the cell. Let's start by adding the code that will target the image in the cell like we did for the Title and Subtitle. The attribute for the images in the cell is called **imageView**. Around line 71, add the following bold code:

    ```
    // Configure the cell...
    cell.textLabel.text = [bandTitles objectAtIndex:indexPath.row];
    cell.detailTextLabel.text = [bandSubtitles objectAtIndex:indexPath.row];
    cell.imageView.image = [];
    return cell;
    }
    ```

    This targets the image in the imageView in our cell.

20. To change the image, we'll use the UIImage class, which has a method called **imageNamed:**. If you pass in the name of an image to this method, it will find the image and instantiate an object. Add the following bold code:

    ```
    // Configure the cell...
    cell.textLabel.text = [bandTitles objectAtIndex:indexPath.row];
    cell.detailTextLabel.text = [bandSubtitles objectAtIndex:indexPath.row];
    cell.imageView.image = [UIImage imageNamed:[]];
    return cell;
    }
    ```

21. Now we just need to pass it a string that contains the image name. We can get this from our bandImageNames array like we did with the Title and Subtitle. Add the following bold code:

    ```
    // Configure the cell...
    cell.textLabel.text = [bandTitles objectAtIndex:indexPath.row];
    cell.detailTextLabel.text = [bandSubtitles objectAtIndex:indexPath.row];
    cell.imageView.image = [UIImage imageNamed:[bandImageNames objectAtIndex:indexPath.row]];
    return cell;
    }
    ```

22. Do a **File > Save**.

INTRO TO iOS *Building a Table View Controller*

3A EXERCISE

OBJECTIVE-C MESSAGE PASSING SYNTAX

In order to accomplish what we wanted with the last line of code that we just wrote, we needed to call two methods: one method gets the name of the image out of the array and the other method instantiates an image based on that name. To make it concise, we perform a **nested method call** where the results of one method are passed directly in as a parameter to the other method. Another way of writing this is to break it up and call each method on its own. Both styles accomplish the same thing, so it is really just a matter of preference as to which style you want to write the code. Below is an example of the alternate code.

The code we added:
```
cell.imageView.image = [UIImage imageNamed:[bandImageNames objectAtIndex:indexPath.row]];
```

Can also be written like this:
```
NSString *myImageName = [bandImageNames objectAtIndex:indexPath.row];
cell.imageView.image = [UIImage imageNamed:myImageName];
```

---

23. Click the **Run** button (▶).

    NOTE: If you get a warning asking if you want to **Stop "Jive Factory"**, click **Stop**.

24. When the app finishes loading, it will open in the iOS Simulator. Awesome! The cells are now being programmatically added using code.

    As we mentioned earlier, the cells are now shorter than what we had in the previous exercise. The custom height of 88 that we used in our static example in the previous exercise also needs to come from the code.

25. Switch back to Xcode.

ableViewDelegate just for this purpose.
us in the code because it is not required and
d it ourselves. Around line 75 after the
method, find this comment code:

ial editing of the table view.

Xcode's documentation. Go to **Help >**

wDelegate and wait a moment for the

UITableViewDelegate.

PAGE 73

Building a Table View Controller INTRO TO iOS

30. Under Configuring Rows for the Table View, click on the method:
    - **tableView:heightForRowAtIndexPath:**

31. There will be an explanation and some code. Select this line of code:
    ```
    - (CGFloat)tableView:(UITableView *)tableView heightForRowAtIndexPath:(NSIndexPath *)indexPath
    ```

32. Hit **Cmd–C** to copy it.

33. Close the Documentation window.

34. After the closing curly bracket around line 73, paste in the code so it appears as follows:
    ```
        return cell;
    }

    - (CGFloat)tableView:(UITableView *)tableView heightForRowAtIndexPath:(NSIndexPath *)indexPath

    /*
    // Override to support conditional editing of the table view.
    ```

35. Now we just need to specify the value to return. Add the following three lines of bold code:
    ```
        return cell;
    }

    - (CGFloat)tableView:(UITableView *)tableView heightForRowAtIndexPath:(NSIndexPath *)indexPath
    {
        return 88;
    }

    /*
    // Override to support conditional editing of the table view.
    ```

36. Click the **Run** button (▶).

    NOTE: If you get a warning asking if you want to **Stop "Jive Factory"**, click **Stop**.

37. Notice the cells are now taller. Congrats on building your first Table View Controller!

38. Switch back to Xcode.

39. Click the **Stop** button (■).

40. Do a **File > Save**.

41. Leave the project open. We'll continue to work on it in the next exercise.

INTRO TO iOS *The Navigation Controller*

EXERCISE PREVIEW

EXERCISE OVERVIEW

In this exercise, we're going to start to create a detailed view for our band information. When a user clicks one of our band cells in the table view controller, they will be taken to a view that lists detailed information about the band. To add this functionality to our app, we will use a Navigation Controller, a common element in most iPhone apps.

1. If you did not complete the previous exercises (2C–3A), complete them now before starting this exercise.

2. **Jive Factory.xcodeproj** should still be open from the previous exercise. If you closed it, re-open as follows:

   – Go to **File > Open**.
   – Navigate to **Desktop > Class Files > yourname-iOS Intro Class > Jive Factory** and double–click on **Jive Factory.xcodeproj**.

LEARNING ABOUT THE NAVIGATION CONTROLLER

Before we add the Navigation Controller to our storyboard, let's familiarize ourselves with how it works.

1. In Xcode, go to **Help > Documentation and API Reference**.

2. Into the search field type **UINavigationController** and wait a moment for the results to appear.

3. Click on the first result (which should be for **UINavigationController**).

4. Scroll down to the **Overview** section and find **Figure 1 A sample navigation interface**.

The Navigation Controller INTRO TO iOS

This is an example of the navigation interface we will be building. What the Navigation Controller provides is easy navigation between hierarchical content. With each controller, you get a title bar, which you can name. In this example the first controller is named **Settings**. When you click on **General** you are taken to the controller which has the **General** title at the top as well as an automatic back button with the name of the previous screen, **Settings**.

5. Now that you have an idea of the functionality we will be adding, close the Documentation window to return to the project.

ADDING THE NAVIGATION CONTROLLER

1. In the Project Navigator click on **Main.storyboard**.

2. We need more room in the Editor area. If you see the Document Outline, click the **Hide Document Outline** button (▣) at the bottom left of the Editor area.

3. Go to the **Object library** (▦) in the Utilities area on the bottom right.

4. Find the **Navigation Controller.**

5. Drag it anywhere into the storyboard except over the existing Bands Table View Controller. It's OK if it overlaps some, but try to minimize it as much as possible. We'll perfect the position shortly.

6. Notice the Navigation Controller comes with two scenes:

   - **Navigation Controller:** manages the relationships and transitions between our views
   - **Root View Controller:** the first controller that is instantiated by the Navigation Controller

   We actually want our existing Band Table View Controller to be the first controller, so let's delete the provided Root View Controller.

7. Click on any blank area of the storyboard so that nothing is selected.

8. Click onto the top or bottom bar of the **Root View Controller** so that it is outlined in blue.

9. Hit **Delete**.

INTRO TO iOS *The Navigation Controller*

3B
EXERCISE

10. As shown below, rearrange the remaining two controllers so that the **Navigation Controller** is on the left and they are lined up next to each other.

SETTING THE INITIAL VIEW CONTROLLER

We need to set the Navigation Controller as our Initial View Controller. Currently it's set to our Bands Table View Controller. The gray arrow pointing to it signifies this. Let's change it to the Navigation Controller.

1. Click on the top or bottom bar of the **Navigation Controller** to select it (it will become outlined in blue).

2. In the **Utilities** area on the right, click on the **Attributes inspector** tab ( ).

3. In the **View Controller** section, check on **Is Initial View Controller.**

4. In the storyboard, notice that the gray arrow is now pointing to the Navigation Controller. Sweet!

SETTING THE ROOT VIEW CONTROLLER

Now that we have the Navigation Controller as the initial view, we need to set the Bands Table View Controller as the root view controller so it is the first controller that users see. We can set this in the Connections inspector.

1. Make sure the **Navigation Controller** is still selected in the Editor (it should have a blue outline).

2. In the **Utilities** area on the right, click on the **Connections inspector** tab ( ).

NOBLE DESKTOP — STEP BY STEP TRAINING — NOBLEDESKTOP.COM

PAGE 77

3B EXERCISE — The Navigation Controller INTRO TO iOS

3. In the **Triggered Segues** section, find **root view controller**.

   NOTE: If you don't see anything under Triggered Segues, click on its name to expand it.

4. Mouse over the **circle** to the right of root view controller so it becomes a **+** sign.

5. Hold **Ctrl** and drag from the circle to the **Bands Table View Controller**.

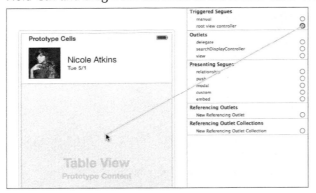

This creates a connection between the two so that the Table View Controller is now the Root View Controller for the Navigation Controller.

ADDING THE DETAIL VIEW CONTROLLER

1. Now we need to add a View Controller that will list the details about a band. In the **Object library** ( ), find the **View Controller.**

2. Drag the **View Controller** so it is to the **right** of **Bands Table View Controller** in the Editor.

3. Position it so it is lined up nicely with the others.

   Now that we have this new View Controller, we need to create a connection between it and the cell in our Bands Table View Controller, so that when a user taps on the cell they are taken to the new View Controller.

4. Hold **Ctrl** and drag from the **Nicole Atkins cell** to the **View Controller** on the right.

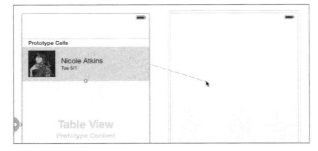

INTRO TO iOS *The Navigation Controller*

5. As shown below, a **Segue** menu will open. Under **Selection Segue**, click **push**.

   NOTE: **Push** is the most common type of segue used with Navigation Controllers. It takes users to a new screen. **Modal** opens a pop-up window on top.

6. Let's re-open the Document Outline. At the bottom left of the Editor, click on the **Show Document Outline** button (▷).

7. In the **Document Outline**, expand **Bands Table View Controller** if it isn't already.

8. Click on **Navigation Item** to select it.

9. In the **Utilities** area on the right, click the **Attributes inspector** tab ( ).

10. Next to **Title**, type **Bands** and hit **Return**.

11. Notice the title bar at the top of the Bands Table View Controller has been updated.

12. Click the **Run** button (▶).

    NOTE: If you get a warning asking if you want to **Stop "Jive Factory"**, click **Stop**.

13. When the app loads in the iOS Simulator, click on any of the band cells. You will be taken to a blank view controller. In the next exercise we'll add band details to this view.

14. Click the **Bands** button at the top left of the screen to go back to the list of bands. Pretty cool!

15. Switch back to Xcode.

16. Click the **Stop** button (■).

17. Do a **File > Save**.

18. Leave the project open. We'll continue to work on it in the next exercise.

INTRO TO iOS *Creating the Band Detail View*

EXERCISE PREVIEW

EXERCISE OVERVIEW

In this exercise, we will create the layout for the view controller that appears when you tap on a band. This view will list additional details about the band you tapped on.

1. If you did not complete the previous exercises (2C–3B), complete them now before starting this exercise.

2. **Jive Factory.xcodeproj** should still be open from the previous exercise. If you closed it, re-open as follows:

   – Go to **File > Open**.
   – Navigate to **Desktop > Class Files > yourname-iOS Intro Class > Jive Factory** and double–click on **Jive Factory.xcodeproj**.

ADDING AN IMAGE PLACEHOLDER, TITLE, SUBTITLE

Let's start by adding placeholders for some detailed info. We'll add a placeholder for an image of the band along with the band name and type of music.

1. In the **Document Outline,** in the **View Controller Scene** section, click **View Controller** to select it.

2. In the **Utilities** area on the right, click the **File inspector** tab ( ).

Creating the Band Detail View — INTRO TO iOS

3C EXERCISE

3. In the **Interface Builder Document** section, **Use Autolayout** should already be checked. Uncheck **Use Autolayout.**

   NOTE: With Autolayout, you can place objects on the screen and have them size/move according to constraints. We're going to start off simple and have elements appear according to where we visually put them, not based on constraints to the vertical/horizontal screen limits (or center). Later we'll use constraints when building an interface for the iPad, but they will be our constraints, not auto-generated constraints.

4. To give you a better idea of the layout we want to create in this exercise, below is the final goal:

5. Let's start by adding the image placeholder. We can use the **Image View** object to display a single image. In the search bar at the bottom of the **Object library** ( ), type **image**

   Image View will be the only object showing in the Object library.

6. Drag **Image View** into the empty view controller in the storyboard.

7. It's too big, so let's resize it. In the **Utilities** area on the right, click on the **Size inspector** tab ( ).

8. Set **Origin** to the top left point as shown below:

9. Set the following (make sure you hit **Return** when you enter the final value):

   X: **20**
   Y: **84**
   Width: **96**
   Height: **96**

10. Let's add a label object for the band name. In the search bar at the bottom of the **Object library** ( ), delete the text and type **label**

    Label will be the only object showing in the Object library.

PAGE 82 — INTRO TO iPHONE/iPAD APP DEVELOPMENT

INTRO TO iOS *Creating the Band Detail View*

11. Drag the **Label** to the right of the Image View object. Don't worry about a specific position yet.

12. Double-click on the **Label** in the Editor, change the name to **Name of Band** and hit **Return**.

13. In the **Size inspector** set the following:

    X: **132**
    Y: **83**
    Width: **166**
    Height: **21**

14. Click on **Attributes inspector** tab ( ).

15. To the far right of **Font,** click on the **Text Menu** icon (T) and set:

    Font: **System Bold**
    Size: **20**

    NOTE: Currently the iOS default system font is Helvetica Neue.

16. Click **Done.**

17. Let's add a label for the type of music. Drag out another **Label** from the **Object library** ( ), and drop it below the **Name of Band** label. Don't worry about its specific position yet.

18. Double-click the new **Label** you just added.

19. Rename it **Type of music** and hit **Return.**

20. With the **Type of music** label still selected, in the **Attributes inspector** ( ), click on the **Text Menu** (T) icon to the right of **Font.**

21. Change the **Size** to **14.**

22. Click **Done.**

23. Let's change the **Type of music** label's text color. In the **Attributes inspector** ( ) to the right of **Color,** click the menu that says **Black Color.**

24. If you see a **blue** color in the Recently Used Colors, select it and skip the next step.

25. To select a blue that matches Apple's blue, do the following:

    – Choose **Other** to pull up the Colors window.
    – At the top of the **Colors** window, click the second tab ( ).
    – In the Slider menu, select **RGB Sliders** if you don't already see them.
    – Select a color with **R:0, G:122** and **B:255.**
    – Close the Colors window.

3C EXERCISE — Creating the Band Detail View INTRO TO iOS

26. With the **Type of music** label still selected, in the **Size inspector** ( ) set:

    X: **132**
    Y: **103**
    Width: **166**
    Height: **21**

ADDING SHOW INFO LABELS

Next we will create labels for the date, time, and venue of the show.

1. From the **Object library** ( ), drag out a **Label** and place it below the **Type of music**.

2. Double–click on the new **Label**, rename it **Venue** and hit **Return**.

3. With the **Venue** label still selected, in the **Size inspector** ( ) set:

    X: **132**
    Y: **123**
    Width: **166**
    Height: **21**

4. With the **Venue** label still selected, in the **Attributes inspector** ( ), click on the **Text Menu** icon ( ) to the right of **Font** and set the following:

    Font: **System Bold**
    Size: **14**

5. Click **Done**.

6. We want to add a label for the date, and it should look similar to the venue label, so let's duplicate it by dragging out a copy of it. Hold **Option** and drag the **Venue** label down to create a copy.

7. Double–click the second instance of **Venue**, rename it **Date** and hit **Return**.

8. With the **Date** label still selected, in the **Attributes inspector** ( ), click on the **Text Menu** ( ) icon to the right of **Font**.

9. Change the **Font** to **System**.

10. Click **Done**.

11. With the **Date** label still selected, in the **Size inspector** ( ) set:

    X: **132**
    Y: **143**
    Width: **55**
    Height: **21**

12. We need another label for the time. The time will go to the right of the date so hold **Option** and drag the **Date** label to the right to create a copy.

INTRO TO iOS *Creating the Band Detail View*

13. Double–click on the copy you just created (the righthand Date) and rename it **Time**. (Hit **Return** to apply it).

14. With the **Time** label still selected, in the **Size inspector** ( ) set:

    X: **191**
    Y: **143**
    Width: **60**
    Height: **21**

15. We need one more label for this top section. Hold **Option** and drag the **Date** label down to create a copy.

16. Double–click the second (bottom) **Date** label and rename it **Age / price** (Hit **Return** to apply it).

17. With the **Age / price** label still selected, in the **Size inspector** ( ) set:

    X: **132**
    Y: **162**
    Width: **166**
    Height: **21**

ADDING A DESCRIPTION

1. Just one more label to go! Drag out a **Label** from the **Object library** ( ), and drop it below the **UIImageView**.

2. Double–click the label to edit the text.

3. Rename it **Description** and hit **Return**.

4. With the **Description** label still selected, in the **Size inspector** ( ) set:

    X: **20**
    Y: **207**
    Width: **280**
    Height: **39**

    NOTE: The description could end up being one or two lines of text. Currently the text is vertically centered within the label area. That would look odd if we only have one line of text sometimes, and other times we have two lines. In a later exercise we'll programmatically set it to vertically align to the top.

5. As shown below, in the **Attributes inspector** ( ) to the far right of **Font**, click the down arrow until the font size ends up as **14**.

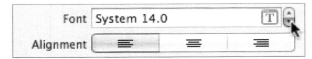

3C Exercise — Creating the Band Detail View INTRO TO iOS

ADDING A DIVIDER

Let's add a horizontal line to visually separate the top info and description. There's no specific object for a line, but we can use a short view as a line.

1. In the search bar at the bottom of the **Object library** (📦), delete the text and type **view.**

2. **View** will be one of the last objects listed in the Object library.

3. Drag the **View** object below the description. Don't worry about the size and positioning, we'll adjust that shortly.

4. In the **Attributes inspector** (🎛), next to **Background** click on the color bar to open the **Colors** window. (If a menu appears instead, choose **Other** and the **Colors** window will open.)

5. At the top of the **Colors** window, click the second tab (📇) to see the color sliders.

6. There will be a menu that says **[Something] Sliders.** From that menu choose **Gray Scale Slider.**

7. To the right of the **Brightness** slider, type in **85** for the % and hit **Return** to apply it.

8. Close the **Colors** window.

9. In the **Size inspector** (📏), set the following:

    X: **0**
    Y: **195**
    Width: **320**
    Height: **1**

Those settings should position the line between the **photo** and **description**. Please note that we're leaving so much empty space below the description so we can add a video, which we'll do in a later exercise.

ADDING THE BAND IMAGES

Let's add one of the actual band images to the placeholder. First we need to add the images into our project.

1. Go to **File > Add Files to "Jive Factory"**. If the menu item is grayed out, click on the **Project Navigator** tab (📁) near the top left of the window. Then try the menu item again.

2. Navigate to the **Desktop,** then go to **Class Files > yourname-iOS Intro Class > Band Images > fullsize.**

INTRO TO iOS *Creating the Band Detail View*

3. This folder contains both the regular images and the Retina versions of the images. Press **Cmd–A** to select all the images in that folder.

   NOTE: You may remember from a previous exercise that Retina images must be twice the pixel dimensions of non-Retina images and end with @2x in their filename.

4. At the bottom of the window, set the following:

   Destination: Check **Copy items into destination group's folder (if needed)**
   Folders: No folders are being added so leave as is.
   Add to targets: Check on **Jive Factory**.

5. Click the **Add** button.

6. In the Project Navigator, notice the files have been added to the main **Jive Factory** folder. To keep things organized, let's move these to the **Supporting Files** folder. Click on **full-ambulance-ltd.png** (or the first image) to select it.

7. **Shift–click** on **full-sleepies@2x.png** (or the final image) to select all the images.

8. Drag them into the **Supporting Files** folder.

9. Click on **Main.storyboard**.

10. Click the **UIImageView** placeholder in the Editor.

11. In the **Attributes inspector** ( ), from the **Image** menu choose **full-nicole-atkins.png**.

12. Let's see how this looks so far. Click the **Run** button ( ).

13. When the app loads in the iOS Simulator, click on any of the bands to view the detail view we just made. Awesome!

    NOTE: Currently, clicking any cell will lead to the same detail view. In the next exercise, we'll show you how to code the app so the details for each of the bands is shown.

14. Switch back to Xcode.

15. Click the **Stop** button ( ).

16. Do a **File > Save**.

17. Leave the project open. We'll continue to work on it in the next exercise.

INTRO TO iOS

Section Topics
SECTION 4

SEGUES PART 1
What Is a Segue?
prepareForSegue Method
Band Detail Object

SEGUES PART 2: PASSING OBJECTS
NSMutableArray vs. NSArray
Creating a Mutable Array
Connecting Band Detail Outlets in Code

TAB BAR CONTROLLER
Creating a Tab Bar Controller
Using an Apple-Provided Tab Icon
Using a Custom Tab Icon

CREATING A LOCATION MAP
Adding the MapKit Framework
Adding a Map View
Setting a Specific Location on the Map
Defining Location Coordinates
Creating a Semi-Transparent Status Bar

INTRO TO iOS *Segues Part 1*

4A EXERCISE

EXERCISE PREVIEW

EXERCISE OVERVIEW

In this exercise, you'll learn what a segue is and prepare it so we can later pass information between views.

1. If you did not complete the previous exercises (2C–3C), complete them now before starting this exercise.

2. **Jive Factory.xcodeproj** should still be open from the previous exercise. If you closed it, re-open as follows:

   – Go to **File > Open**.
   – Navigate to **Desktop > Class Files > yourname-iOS Intro Class > Jive Factory** and double-click on **Jive Factory.xcodeproj**.

CREATING A CLASS

As we did in a previous exercise for the Table View Controller, we need to create a class for the Detail View Controller so we can program extra functionality for it.

1. In the Project Navigator select **BandsTableViewController.m**. (We want the file to be added after this file, that's why we had you select it.)

2. Go to **File > New > File** (or hit **Cmd–N**).

3. Double-click **Objective-C class** to choose it.

4. From the **Subclass of** menu choose **UIViewController** (or start typing it and let Xcode autocomplete it for you).

5. For the name of the **Class,** add **BandsDetail** at the start, so the Class ends up being **BandsDetailViewController** (Notice that is **Bands** plural, not Band!)

   NOTE: UIViewController is the type of object we are currently using on the storyboard. By making our class a subclass of the UIViewController, it will have all the functionality it currently has, plus any additional functionality we add in the code to this new BandsDetailViewController class.

6. Click **Next**.

7. You should already be in the **Jive Factory** folder, so click **Create**.

NOBLE DESKTOP — STEP BY STEP TRAINING — NOBLEDESKTOP.COM

Segues Part 1 INTRO TO iOS

8. Notice a **BandsDetailViewController.h** and **BandsDetailViewController.m** file have been added in the Project Navigator. Now we need to link them to the view controller in the storyboard.

9. In the Project Navigator click on **Main.storyboard.**

10. Select the **View Controller** with the band detail placeholder info (Name of Band, Type of music, etc.) by clicking on its top or bottom bar. It will become outlined in blue to indicate it's selected.

11. In the **Utilities** area on the right, click on the **Identity inspector** tab (🗒).

12. Next to **Class,** type **B** and it should autocomplete to **BandsDetailViewController** Hit **Return** to apply it. Now it's connected to our new class.

WHAT IS A SEGUE?

In a previous exercise, we added a segue that transitions users from the Table View to the Detail View when they click on a band row. Let's read up a bit about segues to see how we can use them to display the appropriate info in our detail view.

1. Go to **Help > Documentation and API Reference.**

2. Into the search field type **UIStoryboardSegue** and wait a moment for the results to appear.

3. Click on the first result (which should be for **UIStoryboardSegue**).

4. Scroll down to **Overview.**

   One basic thing to note is that **segue** (pronounced seg-way) objects perform the visual transition **between** view controllers. Before this transition occurs, a **prepareForSegue:sender:** method is called in the source view controller. It is in this method that we may choose to pass some data to the destination view controller.

5. The **prepareForSegue:sender:** method is a commonly-used method, so Xcode created it for you when you created the table view controller. Before going back to the code, close the Documentation window.

6. In the Project Navigator, click on **BandsTableViewController.m.**

   NOTE: The code we are looking for is only in this file. Take a moment to make sure you're in the 100+ line **Table**View file, NOT the new **Detail**View file!

INTRO TO iOS *Segues Part 1*

EXERCISE 4A

7. Scroll to the bottom of the document (around line 119) and find the following code:

    ```
    /*
    #pragma mark - Navigation

    // In a story board-based application, you will often want to do a little preparation before navigation
    - (void)prepareForSegue:(UIStoryboardSegue *)segue sender:(id)sender
    {
        // Get the new view controller using [segue destinationViewController].
        // Pass the selected object to the new view controller.
    }

     */

    @end
    ```

8. Let's uncomment the code so we can use it. Delete the `/*` around line 119 above `#pragma mark - Navigation`

9. Delete the `*/` around line 129 above `@end`

    Now we will replace the comments inside of the method with some code. To save you time, we already typed it up in a text file for you.

10. Go to **File > Open.**

11. Navigate to the **Desktop > Class Files > yourname-iOS Intro Class > Code Snippets** folder and open **prepareForSegue.txt.**

12. Press **Cmd–A** to select all the code.

13. Press **Cmd–C** to copy it.

14. Close the file.

15. Delete the comments inside the **prepareForSegue:sender:** method.

16. In its place, paste the code you copied:

    ```
    // In a story board-based application, you will often want to do a little preparation before navigation
    - (void)prepareForSegue:(UIStoryboardSegue *)segue sender:(id)sender
    {
        if ([[segue identifier] isEqualToString:@"showDetail"]) {
            NSIndexPath *indexPath = [self.tableView indexPathForSelectedRow];
            BandsDetailViewController *bandsDetailViewController = [segue destinationViewController];
        }
    }

    @end
    ```

    Let's break this code down for you. The **prepareForSegue** method was conveniently written for us by Xcode. Inside this method we wrote an **if** statement that checks to see which segue was triggered. If that segue's identifier is equal to **showDetail** then the code inside the **if** statement is executed. **showDetail** is the name we'll assign to our segue (which we'll do a bit later).

Segues Part 1 INTRO TO iOS

The first line of code inside the **if** statement asks the current table view for the index path of the row that was selected. Index path is how we know which row was tapped. This will help us set the correct info for each band later.

The second line of code inside the **if** statement sets the view controller we are transitioning to, which is **BandsDetailViewController.**

17. Notice the **red error** icon (●) that indicates there's an error in the line of code that sets **BandsDetailViewController** to the view controller we are transitioning to. That's because we haven't imported this class to this file yet, so it doesn't know about it. Let's fix that.

18. Scroll to the top of the code and find the **#import** statement for BandsTableViewController (around line 9) and add the following bold code:

    ```
    #import "BandsTableViewController.h"
    #import "BandsDetailViewController.h"

    @interface BandsTableViewController ()
    ```

    In order for the code above to execute when someone clicks on one of the rows, we need to set the identifier on the segue in the storyboard to **showDetail.** The **if** statement we just added refers to **showDetail,** which is the name we'll give to our segue. Let's set that now.

19. In the Project Navigator click **Main.storyboard.**

20. As shown below, in the Editor, click on the **segue** between the Table View and Detail View Controllers to select it.

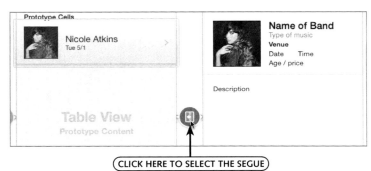

21. In the **Utilities** area on the right, click the **Attributes inspector** tab ( ).

22. Next to **Identifier,** type **showDetail** and hit **Return.**

    The code inside the **if** statement in the **prepareForSegue** method will now execute when this segue happens. Next we can work on passing along the necessary information.

INTRO TO iOS *Segues Part 1*

4A EXERCISE

BAND DETAIL OBJECT

We have quite a bit of information we need to pass along in the segue. The best way to do this is to create an object that will hold all the info for a single band and pass that between the Table View and Detail View controllers.

1. In the Project Navigator select **BandsDetailViewController.m**. (We want the file to be added after this file, that's why we had you select it.)

2. Go to **File > New > File** (or hit **Cmd–N**).

3. Double–click **Objective-C class** to choose it.

4. From the **Subclass of** menu choose **NSObject** (or start typing it and let Xcode autocomplete it for you).

5. Edit the name of the **Class** to be **BandDetail** (that is singular **Band,** not plural!).

6. Click **Next**.

7. You should already be in the **Jive Factory** folder, so click **Create**.

8. Notice that **BandDetail.h** and **BandDetail.m** have been added in the Project Navigator.

9. Click on **BandDetail.h** to open it.

10. Let's start by adding our properties. After the **@interface** line, add the following bold code to add a property for the band's name:

    ```
    @interface BandDetail : NSObject

    @property (strong, nonatomic) NSString *bandName;
    ```

11. We have some more properties to add. To speed things up let's copy the property line we just added. Select the @property line you just added.

12. Copy it.

13. Paste it below the original **nine** times (so we have a total of **ten** property lines).

14. Edit the code as shown below:

    ```
    @property (strong, nonatomic) NSString *bandName;
    @property (strong, nonatomic) NSString *bandType;
    @property (strong, nonatomic) NSString *bandDescription;
    @property (strong, nonatomic) NSString *thumbImageName;
    @property (strong, nonatomic) NSString *fullImageName;
    @property (strong, nonatomic) NSString *nextShowDate;
    @property (strong, nonatomic) NSString *nextShowTime;
    @property (strong, nonatomic) NSString *venue;
    @property (strong, nonatomic) NSString *showType;
    @property (strong, nonatomic) NSString *showDetails;
    ```

15. Do a **File > Save**.

16. Now we need to synthesize these properties. In the Project Navigator click on **BandDetail.m** to open it.

Segues Part 1 **INTRO TO iOS**

17. Add the following bold code after the **@implementation** line. It's one line of code even though it wraps onto two lines below:

    ```
    @implementation BandDetail

    @synthesize bandName, bandType, bandDescription, thumbImageName, fullImageName, nextShowDate,
    nextShowTime, venue, showType, showDetails;

    @end
    ```

18. Count the number of properties you're synthesizing and make sure you have all ten!

19. Great! Now that we've created a class for our BandDetail object, we can create objects that contain the info for each of the individual bands. In the Project Navigator, click on **BandsTableViewController.m** to open it.

20. Let's start by importing the BandDetail class into this file. As shown below, add the bold code after the other #import lines (around line 11):

    ```
    #import "BandsDetailViewController.h"
    #import "BandDetail.h"
    ```

21. To save you some time, we've already written the code that will create the objects for each of the four bands. Go to **File > Open.**

22. Navigate to the **Desktop > Class Files > yourname-iOS Intro Class > Code Snippets** folder and open **band-detail-objects.txt**

23. Press **Cmd–A** to select all the code.

24. Press **Cmd–C** to copy it.

25. Close the file.

26. Find the **bandImageNames** array (around line 40) in the **viewDidLoad** method.

INTRO TO iOS *Segues Part 1*

4A EXERCISE

27. As shown below, paste the code after the bandImageNames array:

```
bandImageNames = [[NSArray alloc] initWithObjects:@"thumb-nicole-atkins.png", @"thumb-ambulance-ltd.png", @"thumb-sleepies.png", @"thumb-black-angels.png",nil];

BandDetail *nicoleAtkinsBandDetail = [[BandDetail alloc] init];
nicoleAtkinsBandDetail.bandName = @"Nicole Atkins";
nicoleAtkinsBandDetail.bandType = @"Rock";
nicoleAtkinsBandDetail.bandDescription = @"Nicole will knock your socks off.";
nicoleAtkinsBandDetail.fullImageName = @"full-nicole-atkins.png";
nicoleAtkinsBandDetail.nextShowDate = @"Tue 5/1";
nicoleAtkinsBandDetail.nextShowTime = @"8pm";
nicoleAtkinsBandDetail.venue = @"Bowery Ballroom";
nicoleAtkinsBandDetail.showDetails = @"All ages - $35";
```

(TO SAVE SPACE WE REMOVED THE TWO MIDDLE BANDS, BUT THEY WILL BE THERE IN YOUR CODE)

```
BandDetail *blackAngelsDetails = [[BandDetail alloc] init];
blackAngelsDetails.bandName = @"Black Angels";
blackAngelsDetails.bandType = @"Rock";
blackAngelsDetails.bandDescription = @"Next year these guys will be selling-out much bigger venues.";
blackAngelsDetails.fullImageName = @"full-black-angels.png";
blackAngelsDetails.nextShowDate = @"Sun 5/6";
blackAngelsDetails.nextShowTime = @"8pm";
blackAngelsDetails.venue = @"Cake Shop";
blackAngelsDetails.showDetails = @"Over 21 - $15";
}
```

Each block of pasted code creates a new object and sets its properties. The first line of code creates an object of the type **BandDetail** by allocating memory to it and initializing it. The rest of the code sets the different properties we created when we built the **BandDetail** class to the correct details for the band.

28. Do a **File > Save**.

29. There is still more to do, but that's enough for this exercise! Leave the project open. We'll continue to work on it in the next exercise.

INTRO TO iOS *Segues Part 2: Passing Objects*

EXERCISE 4B

EXERCISE PREVIEW

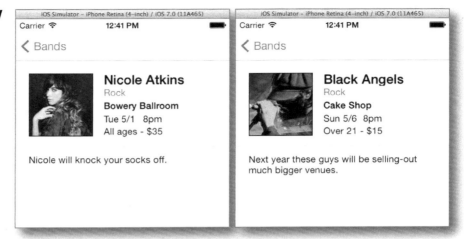

EXERCISE OVERVIEW

In this exercise, you'll learn how to pass data between the Table View Controller and the Detail View Controller via the segue we added in an earlier exercise.

1. If you did not complete the previous exercises (2C–4A), complete them now before starting this exercise.

2. **Jive Factory.xcodeproj** should still be open from the previous exercise. If you closed it, re-open as follows:

    – Go to **File > Open**.
    – Navigate to **Desktop > Class Files > yourname-iOS Intro Class > Jive Factory** and double–click on **Jive Factory.xcodeproj**.

CREATING A MUTABLE ARRAY

We have the objects for our bands created, but we need to be able to pass along the correct object depending on the row the user clicks. If you remember from a previous exercise, we used an array to hold the Titles for the different bands, then pulled the correct band title depending on what the user clicked. We need to do a similar thing for these objects. Instead of using an NSArray, we need to use an NSMutableArray. While they work similarly, NSMutableArray allows us to add or remove objects, whereas NSArray must be populated at creation and can't be changed later. Mutable means liable to change.

First, we need to create a property of the type NSMutableArray in the BandsTableViewController.h file.

1. In the Project Navigator, click on **BandsTableViewController.h**.

Segues Part 2: Passing Objects   INTRO TO iOS

2. Below the **bandImageNames** property line (around line 14), add the following bold code:

```
@property (strong, nonatomic) NSArray *bandImageNames;
@property (strong, nonatomic) NSMutableArray *bandDetails;

@end
```

3. In the Project Navigator, click on **BandsTableViewController.m** to open it.

4. We need to synthesize the property we just added. After the other synthesize lines (around line 22) add the following bold code:

```
@implementation BandsTableViewController

@synthesize bandTitles;
@synthesize bandSubtitles;
@synthesize bandImageNames;
@synthesize bandDetails;
```

5. Now that we have the bandDetails mutable array to work with, let's add the BandDetail objects to it. Find the code for the last band object we created (starting around line 73):

```
BandDetail *blackAngelsDetails = [[BandDetail alloc] init];
blackAngelsDetails.bandName = @"Black Angels";
blackAngelsDetails.bandType = @"Rock";
blackAngelsDetails.bandDescription = @"Next year these guys will be selling-out much...
blackAngelsDetails.fullImageName = @"full-black-angels.png";
blackAngelsDetails.nextShowDate = @"Sun 5/6";
blackAngelsDetails.nextShowTime = @"8pm";
blackAngelsDetails.venue = @"Cake Shop";
blackAngelsDetails.showDetails = @"Over 21 - $15";
```

6. After this code, add the following bold code:

```
blackAngelsDetails.venue = @"Cake Shop";
blackAngelsDetails.showDetails = @"Over 21 - $15";

bandDetails = [[NSMutableArray alloc] init];
}
```

This instantiates the bandDetails NSMutableArray by allocating memory to it and initializing it.

7. Let's add one of our objects to the array. Add the following bold code:

```
bandDetails = [[NSMutableArray alloc] init];
[bandDetails addObject:nicoleAtkinsBandDetail];
```

Here we are using the **addObject:** method to add our **nicoleAtkinsBandDetail** object to the array.

8. Let's add the rest of the objects. Add the following bold code:

```
bandDetails = [[NSMutableArray alloc] init];
[bandDetails addObject:nicoleAtkinsBandDetail];
[bandDetails addObject:ambulanceLtdDetails];
[bandDetails addObject:sleepiesDetails];
[bandDetails addObject:blackAngelsDetails];
```

INTRO TO iOS *Segues Part 2: Passing Objects*

Now that we have an array with the objects we want to pass along, we need to create an object in the BandsDetailViewController that will grab that info. Essentially we need to create an object in the BandsDetailViewController that we can set all the attributes to the same as the object we are passing along.

Because the structure of our app is getting more complex, below is a chart that explains how information will pass through it. Some parts we've already created, and the rest we'll create in the remainder of this exercise.

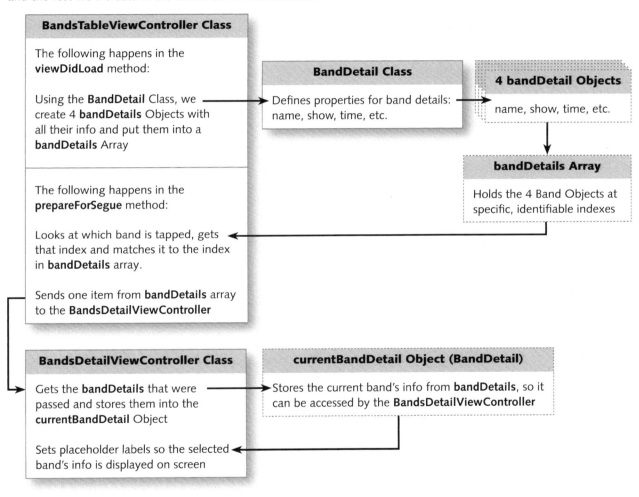

9. In the Project Navigator, click on **BandsDetailViewController.h**.

10. First we need to import the BandDetail class. Add the following bold code after the first #import line:

    ```
    #import <UIKit/UIKit.h>
    #import "BandDetail.h"

    @interface BandsDetailViewController : UIViewController
    ```

Segues Part 2: Passing Objects INTRO TO iOS

11. After the **@interface** line, add the following property shown in bold.

    ```
    #import <UIKit/UIKit.h>
    #import "BandDetail.h"

    @interface BandsDetailViewController : UIViewController

    @property (strong, nonatomic) BandDetail *currentBandDetail;

    @end
    ```

    Here we created a new property **currentBandDetail** of the **BandDetail** type.

12. In the Project Navigator click on **BandsDetailViewController.m**.

13. After the **@implementation** line (around line 15) add the following bold code to synthesize the property we just created:

    ```
    @implementation BandsDetailViewController
    @synthesize currentBandDetail;

    - (id)initWithNibName:(NSString *)nibNameOrNil bundle:(NSBundle *)nibBundleOrNil
    ```

14. Now that we have an object to receive the info, let's send it. In the Project Navigator, click **BandsTableViewController.m** to switch to that file.

15. Find the **prepareForSegue:sender:** method (around line 171):

    ```
    if ([[segue identifier] isEqualToString:@"showDetail"]) {
        NSIndexPath *indexPath = [self.tableView indexPathForSelectedRow];
        BandsDetailViewController *bandsDetailViewController = [segue destinationViewController];
    }
    ```

16. Add the following bold code:

    ```
    if ([[segue identifier] isEqualToString:@"showDetail"]) {
        NSIndexPath *indexPath = [self.tableView indexPathForSelectedRow];
        BandsDetailViewController *bandsDetailViewController = [segue destinationViewController];
        bandsDetailViewController.currentBandDetail = [bandDetails objectAtIndex:indexPath.row];
    }
    ```

    Let's break this code down for you. We are setting the **currentBandDetail** object in the **bandsDetailViewController** equal to the object in the **bandDetails** mutable array at the specified **indexPath.row**. It figures out the correct indexPath.row based on the row that is clicked. If you remember, we set this in the first line of the code in the if statement. Awesome! Next we'll get all the labels in the Detail View Controller displaying the correct info from the object that's passed.

CONNECTING BAND DETAIL OUTLETS IN CODE

Let's connect each of our Band Detail elements with the code so that they will be displayed on the View.

1. In the Project Navigator click on **Main.storyboard**.

2. If the Document Outline is open, click **Hide Document Outline** (◁).

INTRO TO iOS *Segues Part 2: Passing Objects*

3. Make sure the **Bands Detail View Controller** is selected in the Editor area.

4. At the top right of the window, click on the **Assistant editor** button (🎩) because we want to see the **storyboard** next to **BandsDetailViewController.h**.

5. If **BandsDetailViewController.h** isn't showing on the right side, choose it from the menu at the top of the code.

6. You should now have the storyboard showing on the left and **BandsDetailViewController.h** on the right. We are going to create outlets for each of the elements on this page.

7. In the storyboard, make sure you can see the **Bands Detail View Controller** with all the placeholder labels (Name of Band, Type of music, etc.). You'll probably have to scroll over to the right side of the storyboard.

8. As shown below, hold **Ctrl** and drag the **Name of Band** label to the BandsDetailViewController.h file below the BandDetail @property line as shown below. (If you don't see the blue line, you weren't holding Ctrl as you dragged.)

9. In the menu that pops up set the following:
           Name: **bandNameLabel**
       Storage: **Strong**

10. Click **Connect** (or hit **Return**).

11. Repeat this same process for the rest of the **labels** and the **image**, setting the following values for **Name:**

       Type of music: **bandTypeLabel**
             Venue: **venueLabel**
              Date: **showDateLabel**
              Time: **showTimeLabel**
       Age / price: **bandDetailsLabel**
     Description: **bandDescriptionLabel**
      Band image: **bandImage**

4B EXERCISE — Segues Part 2: Passing Objects INTRO TO iOS

12. When finished, the code you added should look like this:

    ```
    @property (strong, nonatomic) BandDetail *currentBandDetail;
    @property (strong, nonatomic) IBOutlet UILabel *bandNameLabel;
    @property (strong, nonatomic) IBOutlet UILabel *bandTypeLabel;
    @property (strong, nonatomic) IBOutlet UILabel *venueLabel;
    @property (strong, nonatomic) IBOutlet UILabel *showDateLabel;
    @property (strong, nonatomic) IBOutlet UILabel *showTimeLabel;
    @property (strong, nonatomic) IBOutlet UILabel *bandDetailsLabel;
    @property (strong, nonatomic) IBOutlet UILabel *bandDescriptionLabel;
    @property (strong, nonatomic) IBOutlet UIImageView *bandImage;

    @end
    ```

13. At the top right of the window, switch back to the **Standard editor** (▤).

14. In the Project Navigator, click on **BandsDetailViewController.m**.

15. Add the following bold code to synthesize the new properties. Write them all on one line of code!

    ```
    @synthesize currentBandDetail;
    @synthesize bandNameLabel, bandTypeLabel, venueLabel, showDateLabel, showTimeLabel,
    bandDetailsLabel, bandDescriptionLabel, bandImage;

    - (id)initWithNibName:(NSString *)nibNameOrNil bundle:(NSBundle *)nibBundleOrNil
    ```

    Now that we have all the outlets connected to the storyboard, we can populate them when this view loads. We want to set each attribute to the corresponding property from the currentBandDetail object that has the info from the object that was passed in.

16. Find the **viewDidLoad** method around line 28:

    ```
    - (void)viewDidLoad
    ```

17. Add the following bold code to this method:

    ```
    - (void)viewDidLoad
    {
        [super viewDidLoad];
        // Do any additional setup after loading the view.
        bandNameLabel.text = currentBandDetail.bandName;
        bandTypeLabel.text = currentBandDetail.bandType;
        venueLabel.text = currentBandDetail.venue;
        showDateLabel.text = currentBandDetail.nextShowDate;
        showTimeLabel.text = currentBandDetail.nextShowTime;
        bandDetailsLabel.text = currentBandDetail.showDetails;
        bandDescriptionLabel.text = currentBandDetail.bandDescription;
        bandImage.image = [UIImage imageNamed:currentBandDetail.fullImageName];
    }
    ```

18. Click the **Run** button (▶).

    NOTE: If you get a warning asking if you want to **Stop "Jive Factory"**, click **Stop**.

19. When the iOS Simulator loads, click on **Nicole Atkins**.

    The detail view will load. It should now be populated with the correct info!

INTRO TO iOS *Segues Part 2: Passing Objects*

4B EXERCISE

20. Click on the **Bands** button at the top left to go back to the list of bands.

21. Click on another band to go to the detail view and see it is populated with that band's correct info as well.

    Notice the description at the bottom cuts off. There should be two lines of description. Let's fix that.

22. Switch back to Xcode.

23. Click the **Stop** button (■).

24. In the Project Navigator, click on **Main.storyboard** to view it.
    (If you don't see it, click the **Project Navigator** tab (■).)

25. Click on the **Description** label to select it.

26. In the **Attributes inspector** ( ), set **Lines** to **2** and hit **Return.**

    NOTE: This specifies the line limit. If the text is longer than the limit, it will be truncated and an ellipse (...) will be added at the end. Setting the limit to 0 would give you an unlimited number of lines.

27. Click the **Run** button (▶).

28. Click on any band (except for Nicole Atkins) to switch to the detail view. Notice the full two-line description is now listed.

29. Click on the **Bands** button at the top left to go back to the list of bands.

30. Click on **Nicole Atkins.**

    Her description is only one line because it has less content. You may remember from earlier that we still need to improve the vertical alignment of the description label. Currently it's vertically centered, so when we have one line of text (like Nicole Aktins) versus two lines (for all the other bands), the space above is not consistent. We can fix this with one line of code.

31. Switch back to Xcode.

32. Click the **Stop** button (■).

33. In the Project Navigator, click on **BandsDetailViewController.m.**

34. At the end of the **viewDidLoad** method, find the line that refers to **bandImage** (around line 39). Add the following bold code after it:

    ```
    bandImage.image = [UIImage imageNamed:currentBandDetail.fullImageName];

    [bandDescriptionLabel sizeToFit];
    }
    ```

35. Click the **Run** button (▶).

Segues Part 2: Passing Objects INTRO TO iOS

36. When the iOS Simulator loads, check out all your hard work. Click on each band to see that you are brought to a view with the corresponding details. The description label text now starts at the top for Nicole Atkins. Fantastic!

37. Switch back to Xcode.

38. Click the **Stop** button (■).

39. Do a **File > Save**.

INTRO TO iOS *Tab Bar Controller*

EXERCISE PREVIEW

EXERCISE OVERVIEW

In this exercise, we'll add a tab bar at the bottom of our Jive Factory app. The first tab will have the list of upcoming shows. The second tab will have a map with the location of the Jive Factory.

1. If you did not complete the previous exercises (2C–4B), complete them now before starting this exercise.

2. **Jive Factory.xcodeproj** should still be open from the previous exercise. If you closed it, re-open as follows:

   – Go to **File > Open**.
   – Navigate to **Desktop > Class Files > yourname-iOS Intro Class > Jive Factory** and double-click on **Jive Factory.xcodeproj**.

TAB BAR CONTROLLER

1. In the Project Navigator click on **Main.storyboard**.

2. We're going to drag out a large object, so let's zoom out a bit. At the bottom right of the Editor area, click on the **Zoom Out** button (🔍) once.

3. In the search bar at the bottom of the **Object library** (📦), type **tab bar**

4. Drag a **Tab Bar Controller** from the **Object library** onto the Editor area, to the left of the current controllers. (Don't worry about the specific position, we'll adjust it shortly.)

Tab Bar Controller INTRO TO iOS

5. Notice **Tab Bar Controller** comes with the main controller (on the left) plus two view controllers (stacked on top of each other on the right) that are associated with two tabs called **Item 1** and **Item 2**.

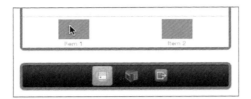

We want the Item 1 tab to be associated with our featured band listings, rather than using the default provided controller.

6. In the Editor, click anywhere on the white background (outside the controller) to deselect the Tab Bar Controller.

7. Click on the top of the **View Controller - Item 1** (the top controller on the right of the new group you just pulled out) so that it is selected and outlined in blue.

8. Hit **Delete**.

9. Click on the **Tab Bar Controller** so it's outlined in blue.

10. Keep the **Tab Bar Controller** selected, but make sure you can see the **Navigation Controller** (the leftmost of the original three controllers).

11. In the Utilities area on the right, click on the **Connections inspector** tab (⊙).

12. Under Triggered Segues, to the right of view controllers, hover over **View Controller - Item 2** and click the **x** to delete it as shown below.

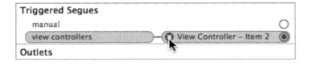

There should now be nothing connected to view controllers under Triggered Segues.

13. With the **Tab Bar Controller** still selected, under Triggered Segues, hover over the circle to the far right of **view controllers**. A **+** sign will appear in the circle.

14. Hold **Ctrl** and drag from the **+** to the **Navigation Controller** in the Editor area.

15. Now we also need to link it to View Controller - Item 2. Hover over the circle to the far right of **view controllers**.

16. Hold **Ctrl** and drag from the **+** to the **View Controller - Item 2** in the Editor area.

INTRO TO iOS *Tab Bar Controller*

17. The two controllers should now have segues from the Tab Bar Controller as shown below:

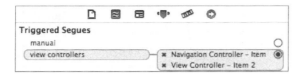

18. Arrange the controllers in the Editor as shown below:

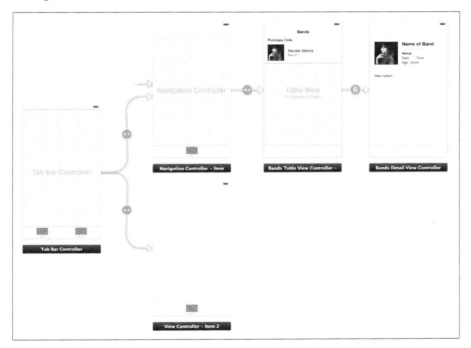

19. To zoom back into 100%, at the bottom right of the Editor area click the ☐ button that's between the Zoom Out and Zoom In buttons.

20. We can have different images for each tab bar item. In the **Navigation Controller** click on **Item** (with a gray box above it) to select it.

21. In the **Attributes inspector** (▦), from the **Identifier** menu choose **Featured**.

22. Notice a **Featured** icon now appears at the bottom of the band listings:

NOBLE DESKTOP — STEP BY STEP TRAINING — NOBLEDESKTOP.COM

Tab Bar Controller INTRO TO iOS

SETTING A CUSTOM ICON FOR THE MAP TAB

There isn't a default map icon, but we can add our own custom icon.

1. Go to **File > Add Files to "Jive Factory"**.

2. Navigate to **Desktop > Class Files > yourname-iOS Intro Class > Icons**.

3. Press **Cmd–A** to select all the images in that folder.

4. At the bottom of the window, set the following:

    Destination: Check **Copy items into destination group's folder (if needed)**
    Folders: No folders are being added, so leave as is.
    Add to targets: Check on **Jive Factory**.

5. Click **Add**.

6. In the Project Navigator, the files have been added to the **Jive Factory** folder.

7. To keep things organized, let's move these to the **Supporting Files** folder. In the Project Navigator click on **locationIcon@2x.png** to select it.

8. **Shift–click** on **locationIcon.png** to select both images.

9. Drag them into the **Supporting Files** folder.

10. In the Project Navigator click on **Main.storyboard**.

11. In the **View Controller - Item 2,** click on **Item 2**.

12. In the **Attributes inspector** ( ) under **Bar Item** set the following:

    – Next to **Title** delete any existing text, type **Map** and hit **Return**.
    – From the **Image** menu, choose **locationIcon.png**.

13. As shown below, you should now see the **Map** icon on the tab bar of the View Controller.

14. We need to change the **Tab Bar Controller** to be the **Initial View Controller** (right now it's the Navigation Controller). Drag the gray arrow that is currently to the left of the **Navigation Controller** (shown below) and drop it on the **Tab Bar Controller.**

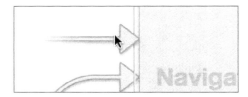

15. Let's preview what we have so far. Click the **Run** button ( ).

INTRO TO iOS *Tab Bar Controller*

16. When the iOS Simulator finishes loading, notice that the list of bands is now in a **Featured** tab.

17. Click the **Map** tab to switch to it. There is no content in the **Map** tab yet, but that's what we'll be building in the next exercise!

    NOTE: The icon we made for the tab bar is black on a transparent background (black indicates the area Xcode will fill in with color). The file was saved as a PNG-24 (called a PNG-32 in Fireworks). The blue coloring added to it when the tab is selected is all done by the tab bar!

    If we wanted to color in part of the Map icon to match Apple's Featured icon, we'd have to provide a second image and do a bit of programming. We'll leave the Map icon as is—it looks good.

18. Switch back to Xcode.

19. Go to **File > Save.**

20. Keep this file open. In the next exercise, we'll get the Map view working.

INTRO TO iOS *Creating a Location Map*

4D EXERCISE

EXERCISE PREVIEW

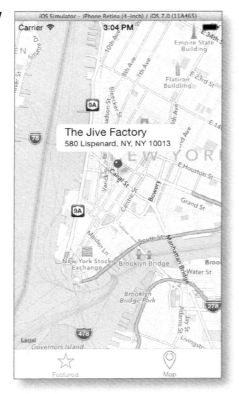

EXERCISE OVERVIEW

In this exercise, we will add a map to our app showing the location of the Jive Factory.

1. If you did not complete the previous exercises (2C–4C), complete them now before starting this exercise.

2. **Jive Factory.xcodeproj** should still be open from the previous exercise. If you closed it, re-open as follows:

    – Go to **File > Open.**
    – Navigate to **Desktop > Class Files > yourname-iOS Intro Class > Jive Factory** and double–click on **Jive Factory.xcodeproj.**

ADDING THE MAPKIT FRAMEWORK

We need to add an Apple-provided framework, called the **MapKit.framework,** to our project. It will give us additional functionality for manipulating the map such as zooming and pinpointing locations. A framework can be a collection of libraries or a collection of code, and it can contain new UI elements or images.

NOBLE DESKTOP — STEP BY STEP TRAINING — NOBLEDESKTOP.COM

Creating a Location Map INTRO TO iOS

1. Click on the **Jive Factory** project name in the Project Navigator. This opens the **Project Settings Editor**.

2. Slightly to the right of the Project Navigator, to the left of General, in the menu select **Jive Factory** as a Target.

   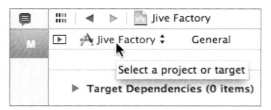

3. Click on the **Build Phases** tab at the top.

4. Expand the **Link Binary With Libraries** section. Here you'll see the frameworks that were already included when we created our project in Xcode.

5. Below the Frameworks list, click on the **Add items** button (+).

6. In the search bar at the top, type **map**

7. In the results, double-click on **MapKit.framework** to add it.

8. In the Project Navigator, expand the **Frameworks** folder (it's near the bottom).

9. Notice Xcode automatically added **MapKit.framework** into this folder. In earlier versions of Xcode, you would have to do this manually. Progress!

ADDING A MAP VIEW

1. In the Project Navigator click on **Main.storyboard**.

2. In the **Object library** ( ) search type in **map**

3. From the **Object library** ( ), drag **Map View** onto the **View Controller - Map** in the Editor area, positioning it so it fills all the empty white space in the view.

4. Make sure the **Map View** is still selected in the Editor.

5. In the Utilities area, click on the **Attributes inspector** tab ( ).

6. Next to **Behavior,** check **Shows User Location.**

7. Let's test this out. Click the **Run** button ( ).

8. When the iOS Simulator finishes loading, click on the **Map** tab.

INTRO TO iOS *Creating a Location Map*

4D
EXERCISE

9. If you get an alert asking to use your current location, click **OK**.

   Because we are using the Simulator, it will not show our current location. On a phone, it will show the user's actual location.

10. Let's test out the zooming. To simulate zooming in the iOS Simulator, hold **Option**. Two gray circles (representing two fingertips in a pinching action) will appear. Click and drag the mouse to simulate pinching.

SETTING THE JIVE FACTORY LOCATION

What we actually want is to show the location of the Jive Factory (not the user's current location). For that we'll have to write some code. First we need to create a new class.

1. Switch back to Xcode.

2. In the Project Navigator select **BandDetail.m**. (We want the file to be added after this file, that's why we had you select it.)

3. Go to **File > New > File**.

4. Double–click **Objective-C class** to choose it.

5. From the **Subclass of** menu choose **UIViewController** (or start typing it and let Xcode autocomplete it for you).

6. Edit the name of the **Class** to be **MapViewController**

7. Click **Next**.

8. You should already be in the **Jive Factory** folder, so click **Create**.

9. Notice **MapViewController.h** and **MapViewController.m** have been added in the Project Navigator. Now we have a class we can work with.

10. In the Project Navigator click on **Main.storyboard**.

11. Select the **View Controller - Map** by clicking on the **battery** icon (▬), giving it a blue outline.

12. In the Utilities area, click on the **Identity inspector** tab (▦).

13. Under Custom Class, next to **Class**, start typing **Map**. Xcode should autocomplete to **MapViewController** and you can hit **Return** to apply it. (If it doesn't autocomplete, just type it.)

14. If the Document Outline is open, click **Hide Document Outline** (◁).

15. At the top right of the window, click on the **Assistant editor** button (▦).

16. **MapViewController.h** should be shown on the right. If **MapViewController.h** isn't showing on the right side, click the menu bar at the top of the file and choose it.

NOBLE DESKTOP — STEP BY STEP TRAINING — NOBLEDESKTOP.COM   PAGE 115

17. As shown below, hold **Ctrl** and drag from the **MKMapView** in the **Map View Controller** into the code below @interface:

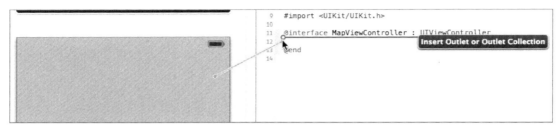

18. In the menu that pops up, set the following:
    Connection: **Outlet**
    Name: **myMapView**
    Type: **MKMapView**
    Storage: **Strong**

19. Click **Connect**.

20. Still in **MapViewController.h,** below the #import statement (around line 10) add the following bold code:

    ```
    #import <UIKit/UIKit.h>
    #import <MapKit/MapKit.h>

    @interface MapViewController : UIViewController
    @property (strong, nonatomic) IBOutlet MKMapView *myMapView;

    @end
    ```

    NOTE: The syntax to import frameworks uses **less than** and **greater than** **brackets <>** and when you import classes you use **quotes " "**.

21. Switch back to the **Standard editor** (🗔).

22. In the Project Navigator click on **MapViewController.m**.

23. Add the following bold code below the @implementation line (around line 16) to synthesize the property:

    ```
    @implementation MapViewController
    @synthesize myMapView;

    - (id)initWithNibName:(NSString *)nibNameOrNil bundle:(NSBundle *)nibBundleOrNil
    ```

DEFINING LOCATION COORDINATES

Now we want to define the coordinates of the Jive Factory to determine where and how much zooming there will be. We need to define three values: **latitude, longitude** and **span** (how far to zoom into the map). We will define these values as constants in our file. **Constants** are similar to variables, except that once the value is set, it won't be changed later.

1. Go to **File > Open**.

INTRO TO iOS *Creating a Location Map*

4D EXERCISE

2. Navigate to **Desktop > Class Files > yourname-iOS Intro Class > Code Snippets** and open **mapCoordinates.txt**.

3. Press **Cmd–A** to select all the code.

4. Press **Cmd–C** to copy it.

5. Close the file.

6. Find the **@implementation MapViewController** code (around line 15).

7. Paste the code above it, as shown below:

   ```
   @interface MapViewController ()

   @end

   #define jiveLatitude 40.72004;
   #define jiveLongitude -74.003912;
   #define jiveSpan 0.05f;

   @implementation MapViewController
   @synthesize myMapView;
   ```

   This code defines three constants: jiveLatitude, jiveLongitude and jiveSpan. To get the latitude and longitude coordinates of an address, you can use a website such as **itouchmap.com/latlong.html** or **latlong.net**

8. Now we're going to use classes provided for us in the MapKit.framework to specify our location. First we are going to use the MKCoordinateRegion class. An MKCoordinateRegion is made up of a center point and a span.

9. Find the **viewDidLoad** method (around line 31).

10. Add the following bold code at the end of the method to declare a region.

    ```
    - (void)viewDidLoad
    {
        [super viewDidLoad];
        // Do any additional setup after loading the view.

        MKCoordinateRegion myRegion;
    }
    ```

    This code created a **myRegion** object of the type **MKCoordinateRegion**.

11. We need to create a center point for our region. Add the following bold code:

    ```
        MKCoordinateRegion myRegion;

        CLLocationCoordinate2D center;
    }
    ```

12. After that, add the following code to set the center's **latitude** and **longitude**:

    ```
        CLLocationCoordinate2D center;
        center.latitude = jiveLatitude;
        center.longitude = jiveLongitude;
    }
    ```

NOBLE DESKTOP — STEP BY STEP TRAINING — NOBLEDESKTOP.COM

Creating a Location Map **INTRO TO iOS**

13. Below that, add the following bold code to create a **span**:

    ```
    center.longitude = jiveLongitude;

    MKCoordinateSpan span;
    }
    ```

14. After that add the following bold code to set the span's **latitude** and **longitude**:

    ```
    MKCoordinateSpan span;
    span.latitudeDelta = jiveSpan;
    span.longitudeDelta = jiveSpan;
    }
    ```

15. Next we need to set the center and span values back onto the myRegion object. Add the following bold code:

    ```
    span.longitudeDelta = jiveSpan;

    myRegion.center = center;
    myRegion.span = span;
    }
    ```

16. Lastly, we need to reference the map view and set the region on it to our region. Add the following bold code:

    ```
    myRegion.span = span;

    [myMapView setRegion:myRegion animated:YES];
    }
    ```

17. Let's test this out. Click the **Run** button (▶).

    NOTE: If you get a warning asking if you want to **Stop "Jive Factory"**, click **Stop**.

18. After the iOS Simulator loads, click the **Map** tab. The map is centered over the Jive Factory's location in New York, but it's missing the location indicator/pin. That's because we still need to create an annotation.

19. Switch back to Xcode.

20. After the code we added to set the region to our region (around line 49), add the following bold code to create an **annotation**:

    ```
    [myMapView setRegion:myRegion animated:YES];

    MKPointAnnotation *myPoint = [[MKPointAnnotation alloc] init];
    }
    ```

21. We need to set three values on this annotation (coordinate, title, subtitle). Add the following bold code:

    ```
    MKPointAnnotation *myPoint = [[MKPointAnnotation alloc] init];
    myPoint.coordinate = center;
    myPoint.title = @"The Jive Factory";
    myPoint.subtitle = @"580 Lispenard, NY, NY 10013";
    }
    ```

INTRO TO iOS *Creating a Location Map*

22. Finally, we need to add this annotation to our map. Add the following bold code:

    ```
        myPoint.subtitle = @"580 Lispenard, NY, NY 10013";

        [myMapView addAnnotation:myPoint];
    }
    ```

23. Click the **Run** button ( ).

    NOTE: If you get a warning asking if you want to **Stop "Jive Factory"**, click **Stop**.

24. After the iOS Simulator loads, click the **Map** tab.

25. Check it out! We've got our location pinpointed! Click on the **red pin** and see that it also shows the title and subtitle we added.

CREATING A SEMI-TRANSPARENT STATUS BAR

1. In older versions of iOS, the status bar at the top of the screen was an opaque black. As of iOS 7, the status bar is completely transparent, which makes the top of our map look much too busy. To fix this, go back to Xcode.

2. In the Project Navigator click on **Main.storyboard**.

3. In the **Object library** ( ) search type in **view**.

4. From the **Object library** ( ), drag the **View** onto the **View Controller - Map**.

5. With the View selected, click on the **Size inspector** tab ( ).

6. If it is not already selected, click the **top left** Origin point, as shown to the right.

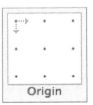

7. In the **Size inspector** set the following:
    - X: **0**
    - Y: **0**
    - Width: **320**
    - Height: **20**

8. Click on the **Attributes inspector** tab ( ).

9. In the menu next to **Alpha** replace any text with **0.9** and hit **Return**.

10. Click the **Run** button ( ).

    NOTE: If you get a warning asking if you want to **Stop "Jive Factory"**, click **Stop**.

11. After the iOS Simulator loads, click the **Map** tab.

12. Notice the status bar looks almost (but not completely) white. To see the transparent effect, move the map around a bit. Our map looks less busy now, giving more focus to the content the users are interested in. Much better!

Creating a Location Map **INTRO TO iOS**

13. Return to Xcode.

14. Click the **Stop** button (▇).

15. Do a **File > Save.**

16. Keep this file open. In the next exercise, we'll link to an external website so that it shows up within our app.

INTRO TO iOS

Section Topics
SECTION 5

LINKING TO AN EXTERNAL WEBPAGE
Creating the Web View Controller
Coding the Link to the Webpage
Adding a Button Linking to the Webpage
Making the Webpage Scale to Fit

EMBEDDING VIDEO INTO THE APP
Adding a Video
Moving the Video to the Band Detail

SETTING THE VIDEO FOR EACH BAND
Adding a videoURL Property
Defining videoURL for bandDetail Objects
stringWithFormat Method

CUSTOMIZING THE APP FOR IPAD
Creating a New iPad Storyboard
Setting the Interface Orientation

INTRO TO iOS *Linking to an External Webpage*

5A EXERCISE

EXERCISE PREVIEW

EXERCISE OVERVIEW

In this exercise, we will learn how to link to an external webpage and resize it to fit the device.

1. If you did not complete the previous exercises (2C–4D), complete them now before starting this exercise.

2. **Jive Factory.xcodeproj** should still be open from the previous exercise. If you closed it, re-open as follows:

   – Go to **File > Open**.
   – Navigate to **Desktop > Class Files > yourname-iOS Intro Class > Jive Factory** and double–click on **Jive Factory.xcodeproj**.

CREATING THE WEB VIEW CONTROLLER

We're going to link to a webpage, so let's make a view to display it.

1. In the Project Navigator click on **Main.storyboard**.

2. Delete any text in the search bar at the bottom of the **Object library** ( ).

3. From the **Object library** ( ), drag **View Controller** onto the Editor below the **Bands Detail View Controller**.

5A EXERCISE — Linking to an External Webpage INTRO TO iOS

4. In the search bar at the bottom of the **Object library** ( ), type **web**

5. Drag **Web View** onto the empty view controller in the Editor, positioning it so that it fills the View.

CREATING A CLASS

As we have done in a previous exercise, we need to create a class for the Web View Controller so we can add the code necessary to go to our webpage.

1. In the Project Navigator select **MapViewController.m.** (We want the file to be added after this file, that's why we had you select it.)

2. Hit **Cmd–N** to open a new file.

3. Double–click **Objective-C class** to choose it.

4. From the **Subclass of** menu choose **UIViewController** (or start typing it and let Xcode autocomplete it for you).

5. For the name of the **Class,** add **Web** at the start, so the Class ends up being **WebViewController.**

   NOTE: ViewController is the object we are currently using on the storyboard. By making this class a subclass of the UIViewController, it will have all the functionality it currently has, plus any additional functionality we add in the code to this new WebViewController class.

6. Click **Next.**

7. You should already be in the **Jive Factory** folder, so click **Create.**

8. Notice a **WebViewController.h** and **WebViewController.m** file have been added in the Project Navigator. Now we need to link them to the view controller in the storyboard.

9. In the Project Navigator click on **Main.storyboard.**

10. Select the **View Controller** with the UIWebView by clicking on its top or bottom bar. It will become outlined in blue to indicate it's selected.

11. In the Utilities area on the right, click on the **Identity inspector** tab ( ).

12. Next to **Class,** type **W** and it should autocomplete to **WebViewController.** (If it doesn't autocomplete, just type it out.) Hit **Return** to apply it. Now it's connected to our new class.

CODING THE LINK TO THE WEBPAGE

1. If the Document Outline is open, click **Hide Document Outline** ( ).

2. Click on the **Assistant editor** icon ( ) on the top right of the window. We want to see the **storyboard** next to **WebViewController.h.**

INTRO TO iOS *Linking to an External Webpage*

5A EXERCISE

3. If **WebViewController.h** isn't showing on the right side, click the menu bar at the top of the file and choose it.

    You should now have the storyboard showing on the left and **WebViewController.h** on the right.

4. We are going to create an outlet for the **UIWebView**. Hold **Ctrl** and drag from the **UIWebView** element in the Editor to the WebViewController.h file below the @interface line (around line 11).

5. Set the following:
    – Connection: **Outlet**
    – Name: **siteWebView**
    – Type: **UIWebView**
    – Storage: **Strong**

6. Click **Connect**.

7. Click on the **Standard editor** icon (▤) on the top right of the window.

8. In the Project Navigator click on **WebViewController.m**.

9. After the @implementation line (around line 15) add the following bold code to synthesize the variable we just added:

    ```
    @implementation WebViewController
    @synthesize siteWebView;

    - (id)initWithNibName:(NSString *)nibNameOrNil bundle:(NSBundle *)nibBundleOrNil
    ```

10. Find the **viewDidLoad** method (around line 27). Here is where we'll write the code to go to the webpage. When this view controller loads up for the first time, we're going to create an external webpage.

11. First we need to define the URL for the webpage. At the end of the viewDidLoad method, add the following bold code:

    ```
    - (void)viewDidLoad
    {
        [super viewDidLoad];
        // Do any additional setup after loading the view.
        NSURL *myNSURL
    }
    ```

12. Next, we need to allocate memory to myNSURL and initialize it with the link to the webpage. Add the following bold code:

    ```
        // Do any additional setup after loading the view.
        NSURL *myNSURL = [[NSURL alloc] initWithString:@"http://www.thejivefactory.com"];
    }
    ```

13. Next we need to put in a request for that URL. Add the following bold code:

    ```
        // Do any additional setup after loading the view.
        NSURL *myNSURL = [[NSURL alloc] initWithString:@"http://www.thejivefactory.com"];
        NSURLRequest *myNSURLRequest
    }
    ```

5A EXERCISE — Linking to an External Webpage INTRO TO iOS

14. Next, we need to allocate memory to myNSURLRequest and initialize it with the myNSURL variable. Add the following bold code:

    ```
    // Do any additional setup after loading the view.
    NSURL *myNSURL = [[NSURL alloc] initWithString:@"http://www.thejivefactory.com"];
    NSURLRequest *myNSURLRequest = [[NSURLRequest alloc] initWithURL:myNSURL];
    }
    ```

15. Now that we have the request, we can tell the Web View outlet to use this request object using the **loadRequest:** method. Add the following bold code:

    ```
    NSURLRequest *myNSURLRequest = [[NSURLRequest alloc] initWithURL:myNSURL];

    [siteWebView loadRequest:myNSURLRequest];
    }
    ```

ADDING A BUTTON

Now that we have programmed the web view to load the webpage, we need to add a button to the Bands Detail View Controller that will transition users to this view.

1. In the Project Navigator click on **Main.storyboard.**

2. Make sure you can see the **Bands Detail View Controller.** It has the placeholder info such as **Name of Band, Type of music,** etc.

3. In the search bar at the bottom of the **Object library** ( ), delete any existing text and type **button**

4. Drag a **Button** and drop it anywhere under the **Description.** We'll position it better in a moment.

5. Click on the **Attributes inspector** tab ( ).

6. Scroll down to the **View** options and set **Background** to **Light Gray Color.**

7. Under the **Button** options further up, set the following:

            Text Color: **White Color**
    Inset, Top and Bottom: **8**
     Inset, Left and Right: **15**

8. Double-click the **Button** in the Editor, change the text to **Jive Factory Website** and hit **Return** to apply it.

9. Drag the button below **Description,** aligning their left edges.

10. We need to create a segue from the **Bands Detail View Controller** to the **Web View Controller.** Hold **Ctrl** and drag from the **Jive Factory Website** button to the **Web View Controller** (which should be below it and contains the **UIWebView**).

11. In the menu that appears, click on **push.**

12. Click the **Run** button ( ) and click **Stop** if you get a warning.

INTRO TO iOS *Linking to an External Webpage*

13. When the iOS Simulator finishes loading, click any of the band listings to go into the detail view.

14. Click the **Jive Factory Website** button.

    This should take you to The Jive Factory website. However, only a portion of the page is showing. At the time of this writing, the website isn't responsive. Responsive sites automatically adapt to various screen sizes such as mobile phones, tablets and desktops. For regular (non-responsive) websites such as this, we can make the page display better by simply scaling it down to fit.

MAKING THE WEBPAGE SCALE TO FIT

1. Switch back to Xcode.

2. Select the **UIWebView** on the Web View Controller. (The **UIWebView** should become a darker blue, but not outlined.)

3. In the **Attributes inspector** ( ) under Web View, next to **Scaling**, check on **Scales Page To Fit.**

4. Click the **Run** button ( ) and click **Stop** if you get a warning.

5. When the iOS Simulator finishes loading, click any of the band listings.

6. Click the **Jive Factory Website** button. The webpage is resized to fit the device!

7. Simulate zooming in by holding **Opt** and dragging on the webpage. (You can also double-tap on any section to zoom into just that section.)

8. Quit the iOS Simulator when you're finished.

9. Switch back to Xcode.

10. Click the **Stop** button ( ).

11. Go to **File > Save.** In the next exercise we'll add a video to our app.

INTRO TO iOS *Embedding Video into the App*

5B
EXERCISE

EXERCISE PREVIEW

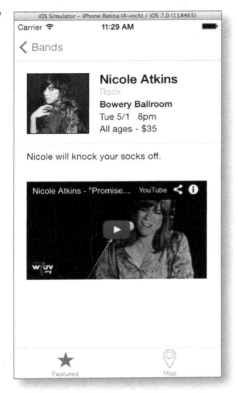

EXERCISE OVERVIEW

In this exercise, you'll learn how to embed a YouTube video into the app.

1. If you did not complete the previous exercises (2C–5A), complete them now before starting this exercise.

2. **Jive Factory.xcodeproj** should still be open from the previous exercise. If you closed it, re-open as follows:

    – Go to **File > Open.**
    – Navigate to **Desktop > Class Files > yourname-iOS Intro Class > Jive Factory** and double–click on **Jive Factory.xcodeproj.**

ADDING A VIDEO

When a user taps the button in the Bands Detail View Controller, we want to load a video of the band instead of taking users to the Jive Factory website.

1. In the Project Navigator click on **WebViewController.m.**

NOBLE DESKTOP — STEP BY STEP TRAINING — NOBLEDESKTOP.COM   PAGE 129

5B EXERCISE — Embedding Video into the App INTRO TO iOS

2. The new code we are adding is going to replace the current code we have linking to the Jive Factory website. Let's comment out those three lines of code. Select the following code (around lines 31-34):

   ```
   NSURL *myNSURL = [[NSURL alloc] initWithString:@"http://www.thejivefactory.com"];
   NSURLRequest *myNSURLRequest = [[NSURLRequest alloc] initWithURL:myNSURL];

   [siteWebView loadRequest:myNSURLRequest];
   ```

3. Press **Cmd–/** to comment out the code.

4. First we need to create a new string to hold the YouTube embedded video HTML code. After the code you just commented out, add the following bold code:

   ```
   //     NSURLRequest *myNSURLRequest = [[NSURLRequest alloc] initWithURL:myNSURL];
   //
   //     [siteWebView loadRequest:myNSURLRequest];
          NSString *htmlString = @"";
   }
   ```

   We'll add the HTML code for the embedded video in between the quotes. Let's get that code.

5. Open a web browser (Safari, Chrome, Firefox, etc.)

6. Go to **tinyurl.com/nicole-promised**

7. Below the video and view count, click the **Share** tab.

8. Below that, click the **Embed** tab.

   Under that, you should see some HTML code.

9. UNcheck **Show suggested videos when the video finishes.**

10. Click into the HTML code and hit **Cmd–A** to select it all.

11. Press **Cmd–C** to copy it.

12. Close the web browser window.

13. Switch back to Xcode.

    We've prepared some code for you in a file to make the video flexible (responsive). Unfortunately YouTube doesn't include this.

14. Go to **File > Open** (or hit **Cmd–O**).

15. Navigate to **Desktop > Class Files > yourname-iOS Intro Class > Code Snippets** and open **flexible-video.txt.**

16. **Paste** the YouTube code in a new line after the existing code. Notice the two blocks of code are similar, but we've replaced the height and width with some code that makes the video flexible.

INTRO TO iOS *Embedding Video into the App*

5B EXERCISE

17. We only need the link to the video from the code YouTube provided. In the YouTube code (that you pasted in at the bottom) select the link to the video:

    //www.youtube.com/embed/Go9k14yrxeQ?rel=0

18. Press **Cmd–C** to copy it.

19. In the code above that we provided, highlight **PASTE_LINK_HERE** to select it (make sure **http:** is NOT selected—we need that to make the video show up):

    ```
    <html><body><iframe style=\"position:absolute; top:0; left:0; width:100%; height:100%;\" src=\"http:PASTE_LINK_HERE\" frameborder=\"0\" allowfullscreen></iframe></body></html>
    ```

    NOTE: Previously, YouTube automatically provided http: in its embed code. Now they are giving developers the choice to use http: or the more secure https:. If you accidentally typed over http:, replace it so the video will be viewable.

20. Press **Cmd–V** to paste the link over it.

21. The code should now look like it does below:

    ```
    <html><body><iframe style=\"position:absolute; top:0; left:0; width:100%; height:100%;\" src=\"http://www.youtube.com/embed/Go9k14yrxeQ?rel=0\" frameborder=\"0\" allowfullscreen></iframe></body></html>
    ```

22. Select the code shown above. Don't select the YouTube-provided code at the bottom, just get the top code!

23. Press **Cmd–C** to copy it.

24. Close the file.

25. Place the cursor in between the quotes in the ***htmlString = @" "** line of code around line 35.

26. Paste the code so you end up with this:

    ```
    NSString *htmlString = @"<html><body><iframe style=\"position:absolute; top:0; left:0; width:100%; height:100%;\" src=\"http://www.youtube.com/embed/Go9k14yrxeQ?rel=0\" frameborder=\"0\" allowfullscreen></iframe></body></html>";
    ```

27. Next we need to load up the HTML string directly into the siteWebView. Add the following bold line of code:

    ```
        NSString *htmlString = @"<html><body><iframe style=\"position:absolute; top:0; left:0; width:100%; height:100%;\" src=\"http://www.youtube.com/embed/Go9k14yrxeQ?rel=0\" frameborder=\"0\" allowfullscreen></iframe></body></html>";
        [siteWebView loadHTMLString:htmlString baseURL:[NSURL URLWithString:@""]];
    }
    ```

    NOTE: While **baseURL** is required, we're not using it so we set it equal to a blank value. If all your links start with the same base URL (such as http://www.youtube.com) you could include it. Then links in the web view don't need to repeat that same base address as well. While we could have used it in our example, we think it's better to see complete youtube.com URLS in the code, rather than splitting them apart.

Embedding Video into the App — INTRO TO iOS

5B EXERCISE

28. In the Project Navigator click on **Main.storyboard**.

29. Double-click on the name of the **Jive Factory Website** button in the Editor, change the name to **Play Video** and hit **Return**. Don't worry about the positioning for now.

30. Click the **Run** button (▶).

    NOTE: If you get a warning asking if you want to **Stop "Jive Factory"**, click **Stop**.

31. When the iOS Simulator finishes loading, click one of the band listings.

32. Click the **Play Video** button.

33. You should see the Web View Controller with a video preview. Click on it to play.

34. After the video starts playing, click the **Done** button to go back to the Web View Controller.

MOVING THE VIDEO TO THE BAND DETAIL

Now that we think about it, it seems unnecessary to go to a whole other view to play the video. Let's add the video directly in the Bands Detail View Controller.

1. Switch back to Xcode.

2. Select the **Play Video** button on the Bands Detail View Controller and hit **Delete**.

3. In the search bar at the bottom of the **Object library** (📦), delete any existing text and type **web**.

4. Drag **Web View** below the **Description**. Don't worry about placement, we'll set that shortly.

5. With the UIWebView still selected in the Editor, in the Utilities area on the right, click on the **Size inspector** tab (📏).

6. As shown below, click the **top left** Origin point if it's not already selected:

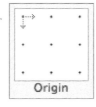

7. In the **Size inspector** set the following:
   - X: **20**
   - Y: **255**
   - Width: **278**
   - Height: **156**

8. Click on the **Attributes inspector** tab (🛡).

INTRO TO iOS *Embedding Video into the App*

9. Next to the very first option **(Scaling)**, make sure **Scales Page To Fit** is NOT checked. The code we provided is responsive and adapts itself to different device sizes, so it will size itself accordingly without the need for scaling!

10. Click on the **Assistant editor** icon ( ) in the top right of the window. We want to see the **storyboard** showing on the left next to **BandsDetailViewController.h** on the right.

11. If **BandsDetailViewController.h** isn't showing on the right side, click the menu bar at the top of the file and choose it.

12. We are going to create an outlet for the UIWebView on this page. Hold **Ctrl** and drag from the **UIWebView** element in the Editor to the **BandsDetailViewController.h** file below the last @property line (around line 22).

13. Set the following:
    – Connection: **Outlet**
    – Name: **videoWebView**
    – Type: **UIWebView**
    – Storage: **Strong**

14. Click **Connect**.

15. Click on the **Standard editor** icon ( ) at the top right of the window.

16. In the Project Navigator click on **BandsDetailViewController.m**.

17. After the last synthesize line (around line 17) add the following code to synthesize the outlet we just added:

    ```
    @synthesize videoWebView;
    ```

18. Now we need to move the video code. We can copy and paste the code we already have from the WebViewController.m file. In the Project Navigator, click on **WebViewController.m**.

19. Select the embedded video code in the viewDidLoad method (around lines 35-37):

    ```
    NSString *htmlString = @"<html><body><iframe style=\"position:absolute; top:0; left:0;
    width:100%; height:100%;\" src=\"http://www.youtube.com/embed/Go9k14yrxeQ?rel=0\"
    frameborder=\"0\" allowfullscreen></iframe></body></html>";

    [siteWebView loadHTMLString:htmlString baseURL:[NSURL URLWithString:@""]];
    ```

20. Hit **Cmd–C** to copy it.

21. Go to **BandsDetailViewController.m**.

22. Find the viewDidLoad method (around line 29).

Embedding Video into the App — INTRO TO iOS

EXERCISE 5B

23. At the end of the method, paste the code you just copied:

    ```
    [bandDescriptionLabel sizeToFit];

    NSString *htmlString = @"<html><body><iframe style=\"position:absolute; top:0;
    left:0; width:100%; height:100%;\" src=\"http://www.youtube.com/embed/Go9k14yrxeQ?rel=0\"
    frameborder=\"0\" allowfullscreen></iframe></body></html>";

        [siteWebView loadHTMLString:htmlString baseURL:[NSURL URLWithString:@""]];
    }
    ```

24. Change siteWebView to videoWebView:

    ```
    [videoWebView loadHTMLString:htmlString baseURL:[NSURL URLWithString:@""]];
    ```

25. Click the **Run** button (▶).

    NOTE: If you get a warning asking if you want to **Stop "Jive Factory"**, click **Stop.**

26. When the iOS Simulator finishes loading, click on a band listing.

27. Now the video should load directly in the detail view. Click it to launch the video. Awesome! In the next exercise, we'll load different videos for each of our bands.

28. After the video starts playing, click **Done** to stop it.

29. Switch back to Xcode.

30. Click the **Stop** button (■).

CLEANING UP

1. Now that we're no longer using the Web View Controller, let's delete it. In the Project Navigator click on **Main.storyboard.** (If you don't see it, click the **Project Navigator** tab (▦) first.)

2. Click on the **Web View Controller** to select it. Be sure to get the controller that's below the Bands Detail View Controller, not the UIWebView! The controller should become outlined in blue.

3. Press **Delete** to remove it.

4. Notice in the Project Navigator we still have the .h and .m files for **WebViewController.** Let's delete them as well. Click on **WebViewController.h.**

5. Hold **Shift** and click on **WebViewController.m** so both .h and .m files are selected.

6. Press **Delete.**

7. When asked about moving the files, click **Move to Trash.**

8. Go to **File > Save.**

9. Keep this file open. In the next exercise, we'll add a different YouTube video for each band.

INTRO TO iPHONE/iPAD APP DEVELOPMENT

INTRO TO iOS *Setting the Video for Each Band*

5C EXERCISE

EXERCISE PREVIEW

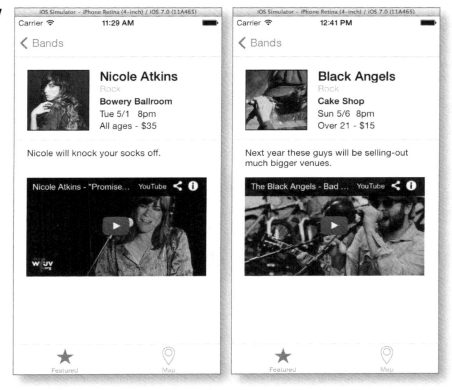

EXERCISE OVERVIEW

In the previous exercise we embedded a video into the detail view, but it's the same video for each band! In this exercise, you'll learn how to pass along the correct video URL, depending on the currently chosen band.

1. If you did not complete the previous exercises (2C–5B), complete them now before starting this exercise.

2. **Jive Factory.xcodeproj** should still be open from the previous exercise. If you closed it, re-open as follows:

   – Go to **File > Open**.
   – Navigate to **Desktop > Class Files > yourname-iOS Intro Class > Jive Factory** and double–click on **Jive Factory.xcodeproj**.

ADDING A VIDEO URL PROPERTY

If you remember from a previous exercise, the details for the four bands are contained in objects of the BandDetail class we created. We want to pass along the correct youtube.com video URL for each of these bands. First we need to add a new property to our class to hold the video URL.

1. In the Project Navigator click on **BandDetail.h**.

Setting the Video for Each Band INTRO TO iOS

2. After the last property declaration (around line 22) add the following code:

   ```
   @property (strong, nonatomic) NSString *showDetails;
   @property (strong, nonatomic) NSString *videoURL;

   @end
   ```

3. Don't forget we need to synthesize it. In the Project Navigator click on **BandDetail.m**.

4. Find the @synthesize line for our properties (around line 13).

5. Add the following code at the end to synthesize our new videoURL property (don't forget the comma).

   ```
   @synthesize bandName, bandType, bandDescription, thumbImageName, fullImageName,
   nextShowDate, nextShowTime, venue, showType, showDetails, videoURL;
   ```

DEFINING VIDEOURL FOR BANDDETAIL OBJECTS

Now that the BandDetail class has a new property, we can add the correct video URL to the four BandDetail objects we created in a previous exercise.

1. In the Project Navigator click on **BandsTableViewController.m**.

2. Find the first **BandDetail** object definition for **Nicole Atkins** (around line 43).

3. To save you the hassle of copying and pasting four different URLs, we've created a file for you with these four objects defined with the new videoURL code for you to copy and paste. Hit **Cmd–O**.

4. Navigate to **Class Files > yourname-iOS Intro Class > Code Snippets** and open **objects-with-videoURL.txt**.

5. Press **Cmd–A** to select all the code.

6. Press **Cmd–C** to copy it.

7. Close the file.

PAGE 136   INTRO TO iPHONE/iPAD APP DEVELOPMENT

INTRO TO iOS *Setting the Video for Each Band*

5C EXERCISE

8. Back in **BandsTableViewController.m,** select all the code for the four BandDetail objects:

   ```
   BandDetail *nicoleAtkinsBandDetail = [[BandDetail alloc] init];
   nicoleAtkinsBandDetail.bandName = @"Nicole Atkins";
   nicoleAtkinsBandDetail.bandType = @"Rock";
   nicoleAtkinsBandDetail.bandDescription = @"Nicole will knock your socks off.";
   nicoleAtkinsBandDetail.fullImageName = @"full-nicole-atkins.png";
   nicoleAtkinsBandDetail.nextShowDate = @"Tue 5/1";
   nicoleAtkinsBandDetail.nextShowTime = @"8pm";
   nicoleAtkinsBandDetail.venue = @"Bowery Ballroom";
   nicoleAtkinsBandDetail.showDetails = @"All ages - $35";
   ```

   TO SAVE SPACE WE REMOVED THE TWO MIDDLE BANDS, BUT THEY WILL BE THERE IN YOUR CODE

   ```
   BandDetail *blackAngelsDetails = [[BandDetail alloc] init];
   blackAngelsDetails.bandName = @"Black Angels";
   blackAngelsDetails.bandType = @"Rock";
   blackAngelsDetails.bandDescription = @"Next year these guys will be selling-out much bigger venues.";
   blackAngelsDetails.fullImageName = @"full-black-angels.png";
   blackAngelsDetails.nextShowDate = @"Sun 5/6";
   blackAngelsDetails.nextShowTime = @"8pm";
   blackAngelsDetails.venue = @"Cake Shop";
   blackAngelsDetails.showDetails = @"Over 21 - $15";
   ```

9. Press **Cmd–V** to replace the code with the prepared code you copied.

10. Find the code where we define the **videoURL** for Nicole Atkins (around line 52):

    ```
    nicoleAtkinsBandDetail.videoURL = @"http://www.youtube.com/embed/Go9k14yrxeQ?rel=0";
    ```

    Notice it's the same as the other string definitions. The code you pasted is exactly the same as what was there previously, except for each band, we added a unique videoURL.

STRINGWITHFORMAT METHOD

1. Now we need to get it so that the correct video is being shown for each band. In the Project Navigator, click on **BandsDetailViewController.m.**

2. Find the code that defines the **htmlString** for the video (around line 44).

   ```
   NSString *htmlString = @"<html><body><iframe style=\"position:absolute; top:0; left:0; width:100%; height:100%;\" src=\"http://www.youtube.com/embed/Go9k14yrxeQ?rel=0\" frameborder=\"0\" allowfullscreen></iframe></body></html>";
   ```

   We are going to be replacing the current youtube.com link with the one that gets passed depending which band the user taps in the app. If you remember from a previous exercise, we use the **currentBandDetail** object to hold that information. There are a few steps we have to do to be able to add the videoURL property to our string. If you remember from a previous exercise, we can add properties to strings using the **stringWithFormat:** method.

NOBLE DESKTOP — STEP BY STEP TRAINING — NOBLEDESKTOP.COM   PAGE 137

5C EXERCISE — Setting the Video for Each Band — INTRO TO iOS

3. As shown below, add the following code to the existing string definition to use the **stringWithFormat:** method.

   ```
   NSString *htmlString = [NSString stringWithFormat:@"<html><body><iframe style=\"position:absolute; top:0; left:0; width:100%; height:100%;\" src=\"http://www.youtube.com/embed/Go9k14yrxeQ?rel=0\" frameborder=\"0\" allowfullscreen></iframe></body></html>"];
   ```

   DON'T MISS THE CLOSING BRACKET!

4. We need to replace the current URL with a placeholder for our videoURL property. Delete the URL and replace it with **%@**

   ```
   NSString *htmlString = [NSString stringWithFormat:@"<html><body><iframe style=\"position:absolute; top:0; left:0; width:100%; height:100%;\" src=\"%@\" frameborder=\'0\" allowfullscreen></iframe></body></html>"];
   ```

5. Now we need to tell it what property to place in that placeholder. Add the following bold code. Don't miss the comma!

   ```
   NSString *htmlString = [NSString stringWithFormat:@"<html><body><iframe style=\"position:absolute; top:0; left:0; width:100%; height:100%;\" src=\"%@\" frameborder=\'0\" allowfullscreen></iframe></body></html>", currentBandDetail.videoURL];
   ```

6. Next to the number on the left, notice we are getting a yellow alert. The % signs in our CSS code is tripping up Xcode. The stringWithFormat: method uses the % sign to start to define placeholders. We need to escape these characters so they are treated as just percent sign strings and not part of a placeholder. The way you escape a percent sign character is with **%%**. Edit the code by adding a % sign in front of the current % sign for the **width** and **height**:

   ```
   width:100%%; height:100%%;
   ```

7. Notice we no longer get an alert. Sweet!

8. Click the **Run** button (▶) and click **Stop** if a warning appears.

9. When the iOS Simulator finishes loading, click on one of the band listings.

10. Pay attention to which video loads in the detail view.

11. Click the **Bands** button at the top left.

12. Click on another band. Notice a different video loads. Awesome!

13. Switch back to Xcode.

14. Click the **Stop** button (■).

15. Go to **File > Save.**

16. Keep this file open. In the next exercise, we'll change our app into a universal app that also works on the iPad.

INTRO TO iOS *Customizing the App for iPad*

5D EXERCISE

EXERCISE PREVIEW

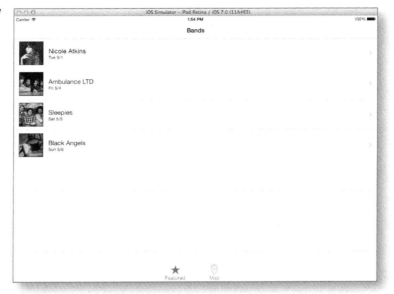

EXERCISE OVERVIEW

The app we've worked with in previous exercises was designed for the iPhone. In this exercise you'll start learning how to adjust the app so it also works well on the iPad.

1. If you did not complete the previous exercises (2C–5C), complete them now before starting this exercise.

2. **Jive Factory.xcodeproj** should still be open from the previous exercise. If you closed it, re-open as follows:

   – Go to **File > Open**.
   – Navigate to **Desktop > Class Files > yourname-iOS Intro Class > Jive Factory** and double-click on **Jive Factory.xcodeproj**.

GETTING STARTED

Before we make any changes, let's take a look at how our app currently looks on an iPad.

1. At the top left of Xcode, click on **iPhone Retina (4-inch)** and change it to **iPad Retina**.

2. Click the **Run** button (▶).

   NOTE: If you get a warning asking if you want to **Stop "Jive Factory"**, click **Stop**.

NOBLE DESKTOP — STEP BY STEP TRAINING — NOBLEDESKTOP.COM

3. When the iOS Simulator finishes loading, notice the app is inside an iPhone-size container. Even though we're running the iPad Simulator, the build settings on our app are specific to iPhone.

   NOTE: You may need to scroll around the window to see the whole app if the preview is too large for your screen.

4. In the top right corner, click on the **1x** button then click on the **2x** button to see it at 2x again. Notice that it appears to be low-resolution. That's because, as we mentioned, it's set for iPhone size. The 2x button just scales up the app. While the app functions, we can make it a lot better than this.

5. Switch back to Xcode.

   We want to create a universal app for both iPhone and iPad. We can actually use the code that we've written so far for both by making a few changes.

6. Click the **Project Navigator** tab ( ) if you're not already in it.

7. In the Project Navigator, click on the **Jive Factory** project name to open the **Project Settings Editor** (on the right).

8. In the column to the right of Project Navigator and to the left of the General tab, make sure **Jive Factory** is selected.

9. If you are not in the **General** tab, click on it at the top.

10. In the **Deployment Info** section, from the **Devices** menu, change **iPhone** to **Universal**.

11. In the dialog that asks if you'd like to copy 'Main' to use as the main iPad interface, click the **Don't Copy** button.

12. Let's see what that did. Click the **Run** button ( ) and click **Stop** if needed.

13. When the iOS Simulator finishes loading, notice the app now displays in the iPad layout. Cool!

14. At the bottom, click on the **Map** tab (if you can't see the Map tab, scroll down or choose **Window > Scale > 50%**).

15. The status bar background at the top is still iPhone size, but the map is already working! At the bottom, click on the **Featured** tab.

INTRO TO iOS *Customizing the App for iPad*

EXERCISE 5D

16. Click on one of the bands to go into the detail view. Whoa! Not so cool...

    As you can see, the content positioning (such as the text layout) is still designed for the iPhone. We also have some issues with the image scaling up. With the wider screen size, we really need to rethink how we are laying out this app on the iPad. What we need to do is create a new layout for the iPad that takes advantage of the extra screen space.

17. Switch back to Xcode.

NEW IPAD STORYBOARD

Within the project, we're going to create a new storyboard, specifically for the iPad layout, so that we can leave our original storyboard for iPhone as is.

1. In the Project Navigator click on **Main.storyboard.** (We want the new storyboard to come after this file.)

2. Hit **Cmd–N** to open a new file.

3. In the template dialog, in the left column under **iOS**, click on **User Interface**.

4. In the main section of the dialog, double-click on **Storyboard**.

5. From the **Device Family** menu, choose **iPad**.

6. Click **Next**.

7. Next to **Save As,** type **Main_iPad.storyboard**

8. You should be in the **Jive Factory** folder so click **Create**.

9. Let's copy all the elements from the original iPhone storyboard to our new iPad storyboard. In the Project Navigator click on **Main.storyboard.**

10. If the Document Outline is open, click **Hide Document Outline** (▣).

11. If the Debug area is open, click the **Hide the Debug area** button (▣) at the top right corner.

12. Click onto a blank area of the Editor and press **Cmd–A** to select all.

13. Press **Cmd–C** to copy.

14. In the Project Navigator click on **Main_iPad.storyboard.**

15. Click onto an empty area of the Editor and hit **Cmd–V** to paste.

16. Click the **Hide Document Outline** button (▣).

17. Click the **Zoom Out** button (🔍) once or twice so you can see everything.

18. All the controllers were automatically converted to iPad size on this storyboard! As shown below, arrange the controllers so that they have the same setup as the iPhone storyboard:

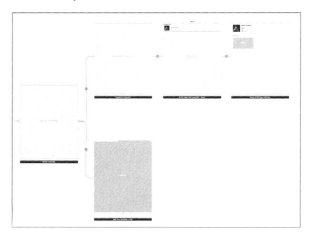

19. In the Utilities area on the right, click on the **File inspector** tab ( ).

20. Uncheck **Use Autolayout**.

21. Now that we have the iPad storyboard, we need to tell the Xcode project to use it for the iPad. In the Project Navigator, click on the **Jive Factory** project name to open the **Project Settings Editor**.

22. In the **General** tab, scroll down to the **Deployment Info** section. Make sure Devices is set to Universal and click the **iPad** tab.

23. From the **Main Interface** menu, choose **Main_iPad**.

24. Click the **Run** button ( ) and click **Stop** if a warning appears.

25. When the iOS Simulator finishes loading, click on a band to go to the detail view. Notice the image looks much better, but the layout could still use work.

26. Switch back to Xcode.

27. Click the **Stop** button ( ).

SETTING THE INTERFACE ORIENTATION

For the iPad, it would be nice if we had the bands listed on the left, and when one is tapped, the details would load on the right. In the next exercise, we're going to use something called a split view controller to do this. The split view controller works best on a landscape orientation, so we're going to lock the iPad into landscape orientation. While we're at it, let's also lock the iPhone into portrait orientation because our app wasn't designed for landscape on the iPhone.

1. You should still be in the **Project Settings Editor**. If not, in the Project Navigator click on the **Jive Factory** project name to open the **Project Settings Editor**.

INTRO TO iOS *Customizing the App for iPad*

EXERCISE

2. First let's set the iPhone. Under Devices, click the **iPhone** tab.

3. In the **Device Orientation** section, we only want **Portrait** to be checked. If any other orientations are checked, click on the check boxes to turn them off.

4. Now for the iPad. Click the **iPad** tab.

5. Click the appropriate orientations on or off so only **Landscape Left** and **Landscape Right** are checked.

6. Click the **Run** button (▶) and click **Stop** if a warning appears.

    When the iOS Simulator finishes loading, notice the iPad app defaults to landscape orientation!

7. Choose **Hardware > Rotate Right** to see that it won't switch even when the device is rotated (which is what we want for this app).

8. Choose **Hardware > Rotate Left** to switch back to normal.

9. Switch back to Xcode.

10. Click the **Stop** button (■).

11. In the Project Navigator, click on **Main_iPad.storyboard.**

12. Notice the controllers still appear as portrait. Let's change them to landscape mode. Select the **Tab Bar Controller.** It should be the leftmost controller, which has two segue arrows extending from it to other controllers.

13. In the Utilities area, click on the **Attributes inspector** tab ( ).

14. From the **Orientation** menu, select **Landscape.**

    Notice all the controllers connected to the Tab Bar Controller have also switched to landscape mode!

15. The controllers are probably overlapping. Move them apart so they have some space between them and no longer overlap.

16. Go to **File > Save.**

17. Keep this file open. In the next exercise, we'll make the app look more suitable for the iPad by adjusting the UI and adding a kind of view controller that is only available for the iPad.

INTRO TO iOS

Section Topics
SECTION 6

CREATING THE SPLIT VIEW CONTROLLER
Adding a Split View Controller
Connecting and Reordering the View Controllers

PROGRAMMING THE SPLIT VIEW CONTROLLER
Connecting the Master and Detail View Controllers
Setting an Initial Detail View
Using the viewDidAppear Method

FIXING THE IPAD LAYOUT
Fixing the Detail View for iPad
Finding Elements that Seem to Have Disappeared

APP SETTINGS: ICONS & LAUNCH IMAGES
Preparing the Assets
Adding App Icons & Launch Images

INTRO TO iOS *Creating the Split View Controller*

6A EXERCISE

EXERCISE PREVIEW

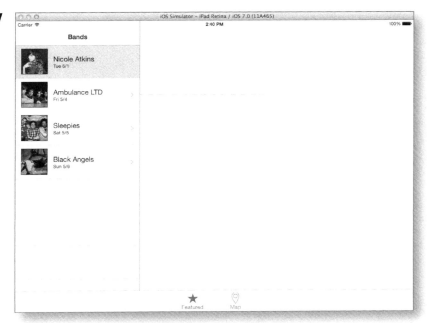

EXERCISE OVERVIEW

In this exercise, we will learn how to create a Split View Controller, a view that only works in iPad apps.

1. If you did not complete the previous exercises (2C–5D), complete them now before starting this exercise.

2. **Jive Factory.xcodeproj** should still be open from the previous exercise. If you closed it, re-open as follows:

   – Go to **File > Open**.
   – Navigate to **Desktop > Class Files > yourname-iOS Intro Class > Jive Factory** and double–click on **Jive Factory.xcodeproj**.

ADDING A SPLIT VIEW CONTROLLER

1. In the Project Navigator, click on **Main_iPad.storyboard**.

2. If the Document Outline is open, click **Hide Document Outline** (▣).

3. Click the **Zoom Out** button (🔍) once or twice so you can see everything.

4. At the bottom of the **Object library** (📦) search for **split**.

5. From the **Object library** (📦), drag a **Split View Controller** onto the Editor area above the **Tab Bar Controller** (which should be the leftmost controller that has two segue arrows coming out of it).

6. **Zoom In** (🔍) on the **Split View Controller** you just added.

NOBLE DESKTOP — STEP BY STEP TRAINING — NOBLEDESKTOP.COM   PAGE 147

6A EXERCISE — Creating the Split View Controller   INTRO TO iOS

7. Notice it comes with the main **Split View Controller** as well as a Master View (the **Navigation Controller** and **Table View Controller**) and a (Detail) **View Controller**.

8. We only need the main **Split View Controller** (which is on the left). Click into a blank area of the Editor to deselect all.

9. To delete the three views on the right, click on one of the narrow views on top (either **Navigation Controller** or **Table View Controller**).

10. Hold **Shift** and click on the other narrow view (either **Navigation Controller** or **Table View Controller**).

11. Hold **Shift** and click on the larger view below **(View Controller)**.

12. With those three views selected, hit **Delete**.

13. As shown below, drag the **Split View Controller** so it's better positioned above the **Tab Bar Controller**.

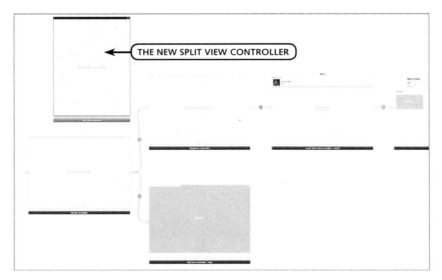

CONNECTING AND REORDERING THE VIEW CONTROLLERS

1. In the Editor, make sure you can see both the **Navigation Controller** (with the **Featured** icon on its tab bar) and the new **Split View Controller**.

2. Select the **Split View Controller**. (It shouldn't be connected to anything now.)

3. In the Utilities area, click on the **Connections inspector** tab (⊕).

4. Under Triggered Segues, hover over the circle to the far right of **master view controller**. A + sign will appear in the circle.

5. Drag from the + to the **Navigation Controller** (with the **Featured** icon on its tab bar) in the Editor area.

PAGE 148   INTRO TO iPHONE/iPAD APP DEVELOPMENT

INTRO TO iOS *Creating the Split View Controller*

6. If needed, scroll over in the Editor so you can see the **Bands Table View Controller** and the **Bands Detail View Controller** have resized. That indicates these will be displayed on the left side of the Split View Controller. (Don't worry about repositioning them in the Editor yet, we'll clean up the arrangement later.)

7. In the Editor make sure you can see the **Bands Detail View Controller**. It has the **Name of Band** and other info on it, and it should be the rightmost controller.

8. We don't want the **Bands Detail View Controller** to be displayed on the left side. We want this to be displayed on the right side. With the **Split View Controller** still selected, under Triggered Segues, hover over the circle to the far right of **detail view controller.** A + sign will appear in the circle.

9. Drag from the + to the **Bands Detail View Controller** in the Editor area. You'll notice the size will change, and it is large once again.

10. Select the **Tab Bar Controller.** It should be to the far left, under the Split View Controller.

11. In the **Connections inspector** ( ) notice that under Triggered Segues, **view controllers** is connected to two controllers currently: **Navigation Controller** and **Map View Controller - Map.**

12. We want to add the new Split View Controller to this list, but we need to add the View Controllers in the order that we want their tabs to appear in. Because we want to add the Split View Controller at the top of the list, we need to delete the connections to all the controllers and re-add them all in the preferred order. Click the **x** to the left of each of the following to **delete** them:
    – Navigation Controller
    – Map View Controller - Map

13. With the **Tab Bar Controller** still selected, under Triggered Segues, hover over the circle to the far right of **view controllers.** A + sign will appear in the circle.

14. Drag from the + to the **Split View Controller.**

15. Make sure you can see the **Map View Controller.** It should be to the lower right of the **Tab Bar Controller.**

16. With the **Tab Bar Controller** still selected, under Triggered Segues, hover over the circle to the far right of **view controllers.** A + sign will appear in the circle.

17. Drag from the + to the **Map View Controller.**

    NOTE: We don't need to add the Navigation Controller because it's now part of the Split View Controller.

18. The **Triggered Segues** section in the Connections inspector should now look like this:

FIXING THE TAB BAR ICON

We need to add the custom tab bar icon for the Split View Controller.

1. **Zoom In** (🔍) on the **Split View Controller** in the Editor.

2. Click on its tab bar icon (**Item** with a square above it) so it gets highlighted in blue.

3. In the Utilities area, click on the **Attributes inspector** tab (▼).

4. From the **Identifier** menu choose **Featured.**

5. Click the **Run** button (▶) and hit **Stop** if a warning appears.

6. When the iOS Simulator finishes loading, you should now see the Split View Controller for our app! Notice the Table View is on the left, but only the divider line is showing in the Detail View on the right. We'll fix the issue with the Detail View band content not displaying in the next exercise.

7. Click on one of the bands and notice the **Detail View** loads in the same place. Even though we set the **Detail View Controller** to be on the right, we still have a segue in the project doing this transition here.

8. Switch back to Xcode.

9. As shown below, click on the segue (gray arrow) between the **Bands Table View Controller** and the **Bands Detail View Controller** to select it. (Make sure you don't select the one from the Split View Controller.)

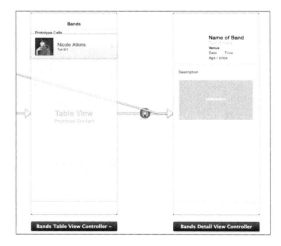

INTRO TO iOS *Creating the Split View Controller*

10. Hit **Delete** to remove the segue.

11. Click the **Run** button (▶) and click **Stop** if a warning appears.

12. When the iOS Simulator finishes loading, click on one of the band rows. Notice we don't transition to our Detail View Controller here anymore. In the next exercise, we'll get the Detail View info displaying properly on the right.

13. Switch back to Xcode.

14. Click the **Stop** button (■).

CLEANING UP THE LAYOUT OF THE CONTROLLERS

1. As we've been working, the layout of the controllers in the Editor has gotten a bit messy. Rearrange the controllers into a layout that makes sense. We recommend a layout like the one shown below.

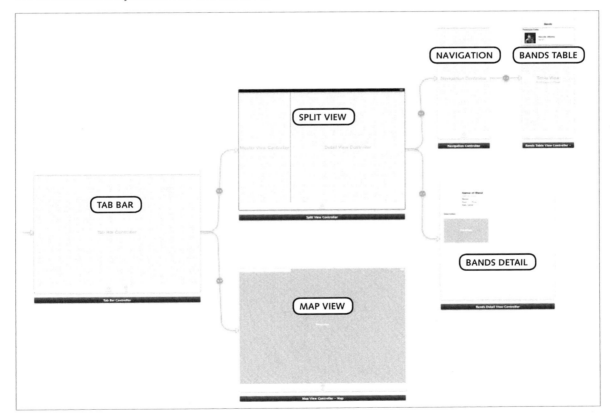

2. When done, go to **File > Save**.

3. Leave the project open—we'll continue working on it in the next exercise.

INTRO TO iOS *Programming the Split View Controller*

6B EXERCISE

EXERCISE PREVIEW

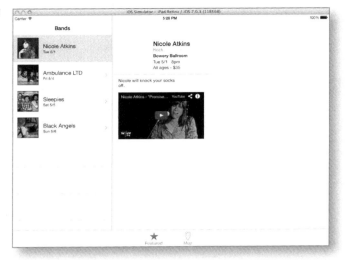

EXERCISE OVERVIEW

In the previous exercise we created a Split View Controller, but it's not finished. When you tap on a band, the details should be displayed on the right. In this exercise, you'll learn how to program that functionality.

1. If you did not complete the previous exercises (2C–6A), complete them now before starting this exercise.

2. **Jive Factory.xcodeproj** should still be open from the previous exercise. If you closed it, re-open as follows:

   – Go to **File > Open**.
   – Navigate to **Desktop > Class Files > yourname-iOS Intro Class > Jive Factory** and double–click on **Jive Factory.xcodeproj**.

SETTING IPAD ONLY CODE

1. In the Project Navigator, click on **BandsTableViewController.m**.

2. Find the code for the **prepareForSegue:sender:** method (around line 175).

   If you remember from a previous exercise, the **prepareForSegue:sender:** method is called when we segue from the Table View Controller to the Bands Detail View Controller. We use this method to pass along the information for each band to the Table View Controller. The segue was also responsible for displaying the Detail View Controller. We don't have this segue in our iPad storyboard, so this method is never called. We need to find another way to display the Detail View Controller and pass along the details for each band.

3. We need to add a method. Go to **Help > Documentation and API Reference**.

4. Into the search field, type **tableView:didSelectRowAtIndexPath:** and wait a moment for the results to appear.

NOBLE DESKTOP — STEP BY STEP TRAINING — NOBLEDESKTOP.COM

Programming the Split View Controller INTRO TO iOS

5. Click on the first result (for **tableView:didSelectRowAtIndexPath:**).

6. Select this line of code:

   ```
   - (void)tableView:(UITableView *)tableView didSelectRowAtIndexPath:(NSIndexPath *)indexPath
   ```

   This method is called when a user taps on one of the band rows in the Table View Controller, and will be perfect for passing along the band detail information. However, one important thing to be aware of is that this code is being used for both the iPhone and iPad versions of the app. The iPhone app is currently fine using the segue. We need to add some code so that the code in this method will only be executed if the user is using an iPad.

7. Hit **Cmd–C** to copy it.

8. Close the Documentation window.

9. Around line 174 (between #pragma mark - Navigation and the prepareForSegue:sender: method), paste the code and add curly brackets:

   ```
   #pragma mark - Navigation

   - (void)tableView:(UITableView *)tableView didSelectRowAtIndexPath:(NSIndexPath *)indexPath
   {

   }

   // In a story board-based application, you will often want to do a little preparation before navigation
   - (void)prepareForSegue:(UIStoryboardSegue *)segue sender:(id)sender
   ```

10. Add the following bold code to check to see if the user is using an iPad rather than an iPhone:

    ```
    - (void)tableView:(UITableView *)tableView didSelectRowAtIndexPath:(NSIndexPath *)indexPath
    {
        if(UI_USER_INTERFACE_IDIOM() == UIUserInterfaceIdiomPad){

        }
    }

    // In a story board-based application, you will often want to do a little preparation...
    ```

    Now we have a place to pass along the band detail info for the iPad, but we still need to pass that info to the Bands Detail View Controller in the SplitViewController. Right now, only the SplitViewController has references to both the Master View Controller (BandsTableViewController) and Detail View Controller (BandsDetailViewController). We need to be able to reference the Detail View Controller from the Master View Controller in the code.

INTRO TO iOS *Programming the Split View Controller*

EXERCISE 6B

To do that, we will create a property in the BandsTableViewController class (Master) that will reference the BandsDetailViewController (Detail). We'll then assign the BandsDetailViewController (Detail) reference in a SplitViewController class (which we'll create shortly) and set the property on the BandsTableViewController (Master).

NOTE: Double equal signs == check to see if the values are equal.
A single equal sign = sets a value equal to the other, thus changing the value.

11. In the Project Navigator, click on **BandsTableViewController.h**.

12. Below the existing properties, add the following bold code:

    ```
    @property (strong, nonatomic) NSMutableArray *bandDetails;
    @property (strong, nonatomic) BandsDetailViewController *detailViewController;
    ```

13. We need to import this class. Add the following bold code after the other #import statement (around line 9):

    ```
    #import <UIKit/UIKit.h>
    #import "BandsDetailViewController.h"
    ```

14. Let's not forget we also need to synthesize the property.
    In the Project Navigator, click on **BandsTableViewController.m**.

15. Add the following bold code after the other **@synthesize** lines (around line 23):

    ```
    @synthesize bandDetails;
    @synthesize detailViewController;
    ```

CONNECTING THE MASTER AND DETAIL VIEW CONTROLLERS

Now that we have a property we can use to reference the BandsDetailViewController, we need to get into the code of the SplitViewController and assign its Detail View Controller reference to our new property. To do that we need to create a class and assign it to the existing Split View Controller on the storyboard.

1. In the Project Navigator, select **MapViewController.m** (so the new file will be created after it).

2. Hit **Cmd–N** to open a new file.

3. On the left, under **iOS** select **Cocoa Touch**.

4. Double–click on **Objective-C class** to choose it.

Programming the Split View Controller INTRO TO iOS

5. From the **Subclass of** menu choose **UISplitViewController** (or start typing it and let Xcode autocomplete it for you).

6. Edit the name of the **Class** to be **MySplitViewController**.

7. Leave both options unchecked (**Targeted for iPad** and **With XIB...**). We don't want **Targeted for iPad** checked because it adds some orientation code that we'd rather not have in this case.

8. Click **Next**.

9. You should already be in the **Jive Factory** folder, so click **Create**.

10. In the Project Navigator notice **MySplitViewController.h** and **MySplitViewController.m** have been added.

11. In the Project Navigator click on **Main_iPad.storyboard**.

12. Select the **Split View Controller** so that it's outlined in blue.

13. In the Utilities area, click on the **Identity inspector** tab ( ).

14. Next to **Class**, type **M** and it should autocomplete to **MySplitViewController**. Hit **Return** to apply it. Now it's connected to the new class.

15. In the Project Navigator click on **MySplitViewController.m**.

16. Find the **viewDidLoad** method around line 26.

17. To save you some typing, we've already written the code that sets the views in split view. Go to **File > Open**.

18. Navigate to the **Desktop > Class Files > yourname-iOS Intro Class > Code Snippets** and open the file **splitViewConnectMasterDetail.txt**.

19. Press **Cmd–A** to select all the code.

20. Press **Cmd–C** to copy all the code.

21. Close the file.

22. Paste the code after the comment in the **viewDidLoad** method:

```
- (void)viewDidLoad
{
    [super viewDidLoad];
    // Do any additional setup after loading the view.
    BandsTableViewController *masterViewController = (BandsTableViewController *) [[self.viewControllers objectAtIndex:0] topViewController];
    BandsDetailViewController *detailViewController = [self.viewControllers lastObject];
    [masterViewController setDetailViewController:detailViewController];
}
```

This creates a property called **detailViewController** on our **masterViewController** so we can set the current band when a row is tapped. It asks the **masterViewController** to assign the view controller on the right to its **detailViewController** property. That way we can tell the **detailViewController** which band to display after a tap.

PAGE 156   INTRO TO iPHONE/iPAD APP DEVELOPMENT

INTRO TO iOS *Programming the Split View Controller*

The first line of code gets a reference to the bands list (**BandsTableViewController** which we name **masterViewController**) by looking at the list of view controllers belonging to **MySplitViewController** (self.viewControllers) and accessing the view controller at the first position (objectAtIndex:0) which is the **Navigation Controller.** Then we want the **topViewController** (the one in first position) from that (which is the **BandsTableViewController**) so it will be the view displayed on the left.

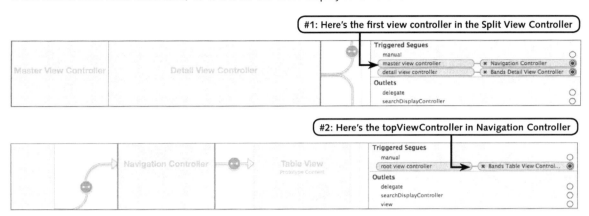

The second line of code does something similar, but it looks at the **lastObject,** which is the position of the **BandsDetailViewController.**

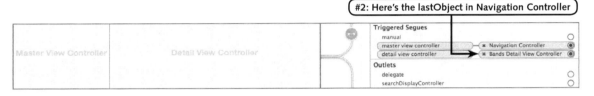

23. Notice we are getting some errors. We need to import the classes for BandsTableViewController and BandsDetailViewController. After the existing import statement (around line 10) add the following bold code:

    ```
    #import "MySplitViewController.h"
    #import "BandsTableViewController.h"
    #import "BandsDetailViewController.h"
    ```

    Now that we're connected to both the Master and the Detail View Controllers in the Split View Controller, let's start working on passing along the band detail info.

24. In the Project Navigator, click on **BandsTableViewController.m.**

25. Around line 177 find the **if(UI_USER_INTERFACE_IDIOM()** statement we added that checks to see if a user is using an iPad.

26. We need to set the **currentBandDetail** object in the **detailViewController** (in the Split View Controller) to the object at that position in the **bandDetails** mutable array. If you remember, **bandDetails** holds the four objects with all the info for the four bands. Add the following bold code:

    ```
    if(UI_USER_INTERFACE_IDIOM() == UIUserInterfaceIdiomPad){
        detailViewController.currentBandDetail = [bandDetails objectAtIndex:indexPath.row];
    }
    ```

Programming the Split View Controller INTRO TO iOS

GETTING THE DETAIL VIEW TO APPEAR IN SPLIT VIEW ON LOAD

There is some other code that worked for us on iPhone, which we now need to change to work on iPad.

1. In the Project Navigator click on **BandsDetailViewController.m**.

2. Find the **viewDidLoad** method (around line 29).

   The view is currently being updated in the **viewDidLoad** method of the **Bands Detail View Controller.** It takes all the values from the **currentBandDetail** and sets them on the appropriate outlet for the view. This worked before for iPhone because each time a row was selected, it used a segue, which created a new view controller. Therefore, the **viewDidLoad** was called and it changed the labels.

   Right now, in the iPad design, we're using a Split View Controller, which only creates the Master and Detail View Controllers once. We're setting a new **currentBandDetail** each time a row is selected, and we need the view updated every time that happens, not just when the Band Detail View Controller is created.

   In order to do this we need to move the code from the **viewDidLoad** method (that sets the band detail info) into a new method we can call anytime.

3. Select the following code within the **viewDidLoad** method (around lines 33–46):

   ```
   bandNameLabel.text = currentBandDetail.bandName;
   bandTypeLabel.text = currentBandDetail.bandType;
   venueLabel.text = currentBandDetail.venue;
   showDateLabel.text = currentBandDetail.nextShowDate;
   showTimeLabel.text = currentBandDetail.nextShowTime;
   bandDetailsLabel.text = currentBandDetail.showDetails;
   bandDescriptionLabel.text = currentBandDetail.bandDescription;
   bandImage.image = [UIImage imageNamed:currentBandDetail.fullImageName];

   [bandDescriptionLabel sizeToFit];

   NSString *htmlString = [NSString stringWithFormat:@"<html><body><iframe style=\"position:absolute; top:0; left:0; width:100%%; height:100%%;\" src=\"%@\" frameborder=\"0\" allowfullscreen></iframe></body></html>", currentBandDetail.videoURL];

   [videoWebView loadHTMLString:htmlString baseURL:[NSURL URLWithString:@""]];
   ```

4. Press **Cmd–X** to cut them.

5. Below the **viewDidLoad** method, create a new method by adding the following code. It should be after the end } of the **viewDidLoad** method.

   ```
   - (void)refreshView{

   }
   ```

PAGE 158 INTRO TO iPHONE/iPAD APP DEVELOPMENT

INTRO TO iOS *Programming the Split View Controller*

6B EXERCISE

6. Paste the code into this new method:

   ```
   -(void)refreshView{
       bandNameLabel.text = currentBandDetail.bandName;
       bandTypeLabel.text = currentBandDetail.bandType;
       venueLabel.text = currentBandDetail.venue;
       showDateLabel.text = currentBandDetail.nextShowDate;
       showTimeLabel.text = currentBandDetail.nextShowTime;
       bandDetailsLabel.text = currentBandDetail.showDetails;
       bandDescriptionLabel.text = currentBandDetail.bandDescription;
       bandImage.image = [UIImage imageNamed:currentBandDetail.fullImageName];

       [bandDescriptionLabel sizeToFit];

       NSString *htmlString = [NSString stringWithFormat:@"<html><body><iframe style=\"position:absolute; top:0; left:0; width:100%%; height:100%%;\" src=\"%@\" frameborder=\"0\" allowfullscreen></iframe></body></html>", currentBandDetail.videoURL];

       [videoWebView loadHTMLString:htmlString baseURL:[NSURL URLWithString:@""]];
   }
   ```

7. For the iPhone app we still need to run this code inside the **viewDidLoad** method. Add the following bold code to the viewDidLoad method:

   ```
   - (void)viewDidLoad
   {
       [super viewDidLoad];
       // Do any additional setup after loading the view.
       [self refreshView];
   }
   ```

8. Let's add a declaration for this method to the **BandsDetailViewController.h** so we can use it elsewhere. In the Project Navigator click on **BandsDetailViewController.h**.

9. After all the property declarations, just above `@end` (around line 25) add the following bold code:

   - (void)refreshView;

10. In the Project Navigator click on **BandsTableViewController.m**.

11. We want this method to run when a user taps a band row on the iPad. Find the **if** statement that checks to see if a user is using an iPad (around line 177).

12. Add the following bold code:

    ```
    if(UI_USER_INTERFACE_IDIOM() == UIUserInterfaceIdiomPad){
        detailViewController.currentBandDetail = [bandDetails objectAtIndex:indexPath.row];
        [detailViewController refreshView];
    }
    ```

13. Click the **Run** button (▶) and hit **Stop** if a warning appears.

14. Click on a couple of the band rows and their info should now load on the right! The picture on the detail view isn't showing up, but that's easy to fix. (We'll fix it and adjust some positioning in the next exercise).

Programming the Split View Controller INTRO TO iOS

6B EXERCISE

SETTING AN INITIAL DETAIL VIEW

You may not have noticed, but when we entered the Split View Controller for the first time (when the app first loaded), there's no row automatically selected. That means the detail view on the right is initially blank. It would be better if one of the bands was selected by default and its details were displayed on the right. We'll use the first row as the one to initially display.

1. Switch back to Xcode.

2. Still in **BandsTableViewController.m,** at the bottom of the **viewDidLoad** method (around line 93) we need to set **currentBandDetail** object in the **detailViewController** to be the first item in our **bandDetails** array when the view first loads. A lot of programming languages start counting at zero, so remember that 0 is the first item. Add the following bold code:

   ```
   [bandDetails addObject:blackAngelsDetails];

   detailViewController.currentBandDetail = [bandDetails objectAtIndex:0];
   }
   ```

3. After that, add an **if** statement to detect that we're on an iPad:

   ```
   detailViewController.currentBandDetail = [bandDetails objectAtIndex:0];

   if(UI_USER_INTERFACE_IDIOM() == UIUserInterfaceIdiomPad){

   }
   }

   - (void)didReceiveMemoryWarning
   ```

4. We want a band on the left to be highlighted, and its details to be displayed on the right. To do that, we'll first need to ask the **detailViewController** for the **currentBand** and match it to a corresponding band in the **bandDetails** array. This will give us the correct index or row. Add the following bold code.

   ```
   if(UI_USER_INTERFACE_IDIOM() == UIUserInterfaceIdiomPad){
       NSInteger indexOfCurrentBand = [bandDetails indexOfObject:detailViewController.currentBandDetail];
   }
   ```

5. Now we need to create an **indexPath** variable for that row. Add the following bold code to store a reference to the current row.

   ```
   if(UI_USER_INTERFACE_IDIOM() == UIUserInterfaceIdiomPad){
       NSInteger indexOfCurrentBand = [bandDetails indexOfObject:detailViewController.currentBandDetail];
       NSIndexPath *indexPath = [NSIndexPath indexPathForRow:indexofCurrentBand inSection:0];
   }
   ```

   NOTE: Table View Controllers may have different sections which can have headings/footers as you scroll through the table view. For example we could have different musical categories of bands. We currently only have one section, which is considered section 0.

INTRO TO iOS *Programming the Split View Controller*

6. Next we'll use the **tableView:didSelectRowAtIndexPath:** method, which tells the delegate that the row we specified (the current row in section 0) is now selected. This will load it on the right side.

   ```
   if(UI_USER_INTERFACE_IDIOM() == UIUserInterfaceIdiomPad){
       NSInteger indexOfCurrentBand = [bandDetails indexOfObject:detailViewController.currentBandDetail];
       NSIndexPath *indexPath = [NSIndexPath indexPathForRow:indexofCurrentBand inSection:0];
       [self tableView:self.tableView didSelectRowAtIndexPath:indexPath];
   }
   ```

7. Click the **Run** button (▶) and hit **Stop** if a warning appears.

   In the iOS Simulator, the detail view should load on the right.

8. While the details for the first row have been loaded on the right, the first row on the left is not initially selected. It should be selected so the user knows which band those details belong to. Switch back to Xcode.

9. Still in **BandsTableViewController.m,** add the following bold code, which tells it to highlight the row we specified as indexPath. It's one line of code, even though it didn't fit on one line below.

   ```
   if(UI_USER_INTERFACE_IDIOM() == UIUserInterfaceIdiomPad){
       NSInteger indexOfCurrentBand = [bandDetails indexOfObject:detailViewController.currentBandDetail];
       NSIndexPath *indexPath = [NSIndexPath indexPathForRow:indexofCurrentBand inSection:0];
       [self tableView:self.tableView didSelectRowAtIndexPath:indexPath];
       [self.tableView selectRowAtIndexPath:indexPath animated:NO
   scrollPosition:UITableViewScrollPositionNone];
   }
   ```

10. In the code you just added, **scrollPosition:** controls what happens if the selected row is not visible (because a list of bands may be so long that a selected row may be off screen). But what does **UITableViewScrollPositionNone** mean? Hold the **Option** key and click on **UITableViewScrollPositionNone.**

    NOTE: If you do not see a full description, you may need to install some documentation. Go into **Xcode > Preferences > Downloads** and under Documentation download **iOS 7 doc set** and **Xcode 5 doc set.**

11. An explanation will appear without you having to open up the help! Read the explanation to better understand this choice.

12. When done reading, click off the pop-up to close it.

13. Click the **Run** button (▶) and hit **Stop** if a warning appears.

14. If you were watching very closely, you may have seen the first row was selected for a second, but then it blinked off and became deselected.

15. Switch back to Xcode.

Programming the Split View Controller INTRO TO iOS

USING THE VIEWDIDAPPEAR METHOD

Currently the **if** statement we're working with is in the **viewDidLoad** method. Although the view is done loading, the table had not finished completely drawing, causing a flicker effect when the row is selected in viewDidLoad. We can fix this by moving the code that highlights the current Band row into a **viewDidAppear:** method.

1. Still in **BandsTableViewController.m,** select the entire **if** statement (around line 96).

   ```
   if(UI_USER_INTERFACE_IDIOM() == UIUserInterfaceIdiomPad){
       NSInteger indexOfCurrentBand = [bandDetails indexOfObject:detailViewController.currentBandDetail];
       NSIndexPath *indexPath = [NSIndexPath indexPathForRow:indexofCurrentBand inSection:0];
       [self tableView:self.tableView didSelectRowAtIndexPath:indexPath];
       [self.tableView selectRowAtIndexPath:indexPath animated:NO
   scrollPosition:UITableViewScrollPositionNone];
   }
   ```

2. Hit **Cmd–C** to copy it.

3. We only want to move the code that highlights the current Band row (the last line of code in the **if** statement). Delete that line of code from this **if** statement in the **viewDidLoad** method so the code looks like this:

   ```
   if(UI_USER_INTERFACE_IDIOM() == UIUserInterfaceIdiomPad){
       NSInteger indexOfCurrentBand = [bandDetails indexOfObject:detailViewController.currentBandDetail];
       NSIndexPath *indexPath = [NSIndexPath indexPathForRow:indexofCurrentBand inSection:0];
       [self tableView:self.tableView didSelectRowAtIndexPath:indexPath];
   }
   ```

4. Below the **viewDidLoad** method you were just working in, you should see the **didReceiveMemoryWarning** method. Above that, add the following bold code for the **viewDidAppear:** method.

   ```
           [self tableView:self.tableView didSelectRowAtIndexPath:indexPath];
       }
   }

   - (void)viewDidAppear:(BOOL)animated{

   }

   - (void)didReceiveMemoryWarning
   ```

   This method occurs every time the Bands Table View Controller appears on the screen, unlike the viewDidLoad method which only occurs once when the Bands Table View Controller initially loads. We want to highlight the row once the table has completely finished being drawn, so we'll use this method.

5. Paste the code into the new **viewDidAppear:** method, so you get the following:

   ```
   - (void)viewDidAppear:(BOOL)animated{
       if(UI_USER_INTERFACE_IDIOM() == UIUserInterfaceIdiomPad){
           NSInteger indexOfCurrentBand = [bandDetails indexOfObject:detailViewController.currentBandDetail];
           NSIndexPath *indexPath = [NSIndexPath indexPathForRow:indexofCurrentBand inSection:0];
           [self tableView:self.tableView didSelectRowAtIndexPath:indexPath];
           [self.tableView selectRowAtIndexPath:indexPath animated:NO
   scrollPosition:UITableViewScrollPositionNone];
       }
   }
   ```

INTRO TO iOS *Programming the Split View Controller*

6. Delete the third line of code that loads the detail view on the right so the **if** statement looks like this:

   ```
   - (void)viewDidAppear:(BOOL)animated{
       if(UI_USER_INTERFACE_IDIOM() == UIUserInterfaceIdiomPad){
           NSInteger indexOfCurrentBand = [bandDetails indexOfObject:detailViewController.currentBandDetail];
           NSIndexPath *indexPath = [NSIndexPath indexPathForRow:indexofCurrentBand inSection:0];
           [self.tableView selectRowAtIndexPath:indexPath animated:NO scrollPosition:UITableViewScrollPositionNone];
       }
   }
   ```

   We only want the detail view on the right to load when the View Controller first loads, not every time it appears. Why you ask? Let's say a user decides to play a video in full screen mode. When they exit full screen mode, the View Controller appears on screen again and the **viewDidAppear:** method runs. This would cause the video to flicker and reload from the beginning, rather than smoothly resizing down and continuing from where you left full screen mode.

7. Click the **Run** button (▶) and hit **Stop** if a warning appears.

8. Finally the first row should be selected, with its details shown on the right!

9. You can see the video issues we mentioned could happen by clicking on the video. Once the video has started to play, hit **Done**. Success! The video smoothly resizes and the thumbnail displays the point where you paused the video.

10. Click on some of the other band rows to see the info changes. We're almost done! (We'll fix some of the layout issues in the next exercise.)

11. Switch back to Xcode.

12. Click the **Stop** button (■).

13. Go to **File > Save.**

14. Leave the project open, we'll continue working on it in the next exercise.

INTRO TO iOS *Fixing the iPad Layout*

6C EXERCISE

EXERCISE PREVIEW

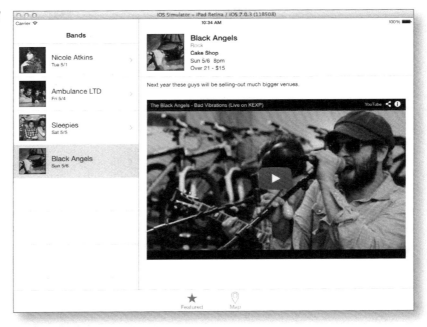

EXERCISE OVERVIEW

In this exercise, we'll finish correcting the iPad layout.

1. If you did not complete the previous exercises (2C–6B), complete them now before starting this exercise.

2. **Jive Factory.xcodeproj** should still be open from the previous exercise. If you closed it, re-open as follows:

   – Go to **File > Open**.
   – Navigate to **Desktop > Class Files > yourname-iOS Intro Class > Jive Factory** and double–click on **Jive Factory.xcodeproj**.

FIXING THE DETAIL VIEW FOR IPAD

1. In the Project Navigator click on **Main_iPad.storyboard**.

2. **Zoom In** (🔍) on the **Bands Detail View Controller.**

   One problem that happened when we copied from one storyboard to another is that the image view seems to have disappeared. In reality it just shrunk. Let's fix it.

3. If the **Document Outline** is not open, click the **Show Document Outline** button (▶).

4. In the Document Outline, select **Image View - full-nicole-atkins.png.** (If you don't see it, expand into **Bands Detail View Controller Scene > Bands Detail View Controller > View**.)

NOBLE DESKTOP — STEP BY STEP TRAINING — NOBLEDESKTOP.COM   PAGE **165**

Fixing the iPad Layout INTRO TO iOS

5. In the Utilities area, click on the **Size inspector** tab ( ).

6. As shown below, make sure the Origin is set to **top left.**

7. Set the following options:

   X: **20**
   Y: **40**
   Width: **96**
   Height: **96**

   The Y position is slightly different from the iPhone layout because we do not have an area under the status bar in the iPad layout. (Because we are using the split view controller, the iPad layout does not have a Back bar that creates extra unusable space under the status bar.)

8. Let's change the Y positions of the rest of the elements to match the photo. Select the **Name of Band** label.

   NOTE: Normally you'd drag the labels into a layout that you like, but because we have a specific layout in mind, we'll give you the exact positions and sizes.

9. In the **Size inspector** ( ), set Y to **40**.

10. Select the **Type of music** label.

11. In the **Size inspector** ( ), set Y to **60**.

12. Select the **Venue** label.

13. In the **Size inspector** ( ), set Y to **80**.

14. Select the **Date** label.

15. In the **Size inspector** ( ), set Y to **100**.

16. Select the **Time** label.

17. In the **Size inspector** ( ), set Y to **100**.

18. Select the **Age / price** label.

19. In the **Size inspector** ( ), set Y to **119**.

20. Select the **Description** label.

21. In the **Size inspector** ( ), set Y to **164**.

INTRO TO iOS *Fixing the iPad Layout*

6C EXERCISE

22. The layout should now look like this (don't worry about the line yet):

FIXING THE VIEWS

Looks good so far, but our line and video web view are too small for the iPad. Let's make them bigger. Let's use the Document Outline to select the line.

1. In the **Bands Detail View Controller** section, inside **View** there is another **View** (above **Web View**). Select that nested **View** (that's above **Web View**).

2. In the **Size inspector** ( ), set the following:
   - Y: **152**
   - Width: **703**

   The divider line now stretches across the entire width. Let's fix the Web View next.

3. In the Document Outline, select **Web View** (you can also directly click on it).

4. In the **Size inspector** ( ), set the following:
   - X: **20**
   - Y: **221**
   - Width: **663**
   - Height: **421**

5. That's better. Let's see how it looks in the Simulator. Click the **Run** button ( ).

   NOTE: If you get a warning asking if you want to **Stop "Jive Factory"**, click **Stop.**

6. When the iOS Simulator finishes loading, notice the layout on the right looks much better.

7. Click on another band row to see the correct info loads for that band. Cool! Notice the band description text is wrapping onto multiple lines. With the increased screen space, we want this description to stay on one line.

8. Switch back to Xcode.

9. Select the **Description** label.

10. In the Utilities area, click the **Attributes inspector** tab ( ).

NOBLE DESKTOP — STEP BY STEP TRAINING — NOBLEDESKTOP.COM

Fixing the iPad Layout INTRO TO iOS

11. Set **Lines** to **1**.

12. Click the **Run** button (▶) and click **Stop** if a warning appears.

13. When the iOS Simulator finishes loading, click on a band to see all the text stays on one line.

14. Click on the **Map** tab at the bottom. Notice the translucent status bar at the top is still too small because it's currently set to iPhone size. That's an easy fix.

15. Switch back to Xcode.

16. In the Document Outline, in the **Map View Controller - Map Scene** section expand **Map View Controller - Map** if it isn't already.

17. Under that expand **View** and click on the nested **View.**

18. **Zoom Out** (🔍) so you can see the whole Map View Controller.

19. In the Utilities area, click on the **Size inspector** tab (▦).

20. Set the Width to **1024** (the size of the iPad in landscape mode).

21. Click the **Run** button (▶) and click **Stop** if a warning appears.

22. In the iOS Simulator, click on the **Map** tab. Voilà! The translucent status bar runs the length of the iPad!

23. Switch back to Xcode.

24. Click the **Stop** button (■).

25. Go to **File > Save**.

26. Leave the project open, we'll continue working on it in the next exercise.

INTRO TO iOS *App Settings: Icons & Launch Images*

EXERCISE PREVIEW

EXERCISE OVERVIEW

Now that our app is functional, we need to finish a few last things, such as setting launch screens for when the app first launches, and icons for the app!

1. If you did not complete the previous exercises (2C–6C), complete them now before starting this exercise.

2. **Jive Factory.xcodeproj** should still be open from the previous exercise. If you closed it, re-open as follows:

   – Go to **File > Open**.
   – Navigate to **Desktop > Class Files > yourname-iOS Intro Class > Jive Factory** and double–click on **Jive Factory.xcodeproj**.

PREPARING THE ASSETS

If you use Photoshop, **appicontemplate.com** has a great template where you can add your icon artwork and it will resize it to all the various sizes and even preview how it looks in the App Store and on the iPhone Home Screen. It even has a set of actions for exporting all the various sizes with the proper names! We used this template when creating the icons for this Jive Factory app.

There are numerous icons of varying sizes. We created a reference page at the end of this workbook that lists all the sizes and when they are used.

Launch images will be displayed when an app is starting up from a fresh state. Apple's documentation says, "Because users are likely to switch among apps frequently, you should make every effort to cut launch time to a minimum, and you should design a launch image that downplays the experience rather than drawing attention to it. Avoid using your launch image as an opportunity to provide an 'app entry experience' such as a splash screen, an 'About' window, or branding elements, unless they are a static part of your app's first screen. If you think that following these guidelines will result in a plain, boring launch image, you're right. Remember, the launch image is not meant to provide an opportunity for artistic expression; it is solely intended to enhance the user's perception of your app as quick to launch and immediately ready for use."

6D EXERCISE — App Settings: Icons & Launch Images INTRO TO iOS

We made the launch images for our app by running it in the iOS Simulator. To save a screenshot to the Desktop, we hit **Cmd–S**. We then used Photoshop to remove user interface elements that could change.

USING THE ASSETS CATALOG

One of the new features in Xcode 5 is the assets catalog which makes managing images in your application much easier.

1. In the Project Navigator click on the **Images.xcassets** folder located inside the Jive Factory project folder.

2. In the Editor, in the column on the left, you should see an **AppIcon** and **LaunchImage** catalog.

3. Click the **AppIcon** catalog.

4. Notice this opens the catalog on the right side of the Editor, with three empty areas for icons as shown below:

Below each empty area, there is a description of what the icon image is used for and the iOS version. The 2x refers to the resolution of the image, and the size of the image (in points) is at the bottom.

5. In the Utilities area, click on the **Attributes inspector** tab ( ).

6. Notice that currently only the **iPhone iOS 7.0 and Later Sizes** is checked. Because this is a universal app, we also want to be able to add the app icon images for the iPad.

7. In the iPad section, check on **iPad iOS 7.0 and Later Sizes.**

8. Notice more empty icon areas have been added for the iPad.

    NOTE: We aren't supporting iOS 6.1 and prior in this workbook, but if you are in your own apps, you would also check these options.

9. Open a **Finder** window.

10. Navigate to the **Desktop > Class Files > yourname-iOS Intro Class > App Icons** folder.

11. Position the Finder window so you can see it as well as the empty icon areas in Xcode.

INTRO TO iOS *App Settings: Icons & Launch Images*

6D
EXERCISE

12. From the Finder window, drag the **AppIcon29x29@2x.png** file over to Xcode and drop it over the first iPhone empty icon area as shown below:

13. Repeat this process for the rest of the app icons, dragging over the corresponding files:

2x iPhone Spotlight iOS 7 40pt:	**AppIcon40x40@2x.png**
2x iPhone App iOS 7 60pt:	**AppIcon60x60@2x.png**
1x iPad Settings iOS 5–7 29pt:	**AppIcon29x29.png**
2x iPad Settings iOS 5–7 29pt:	**AppIcon29x29@2x.png**
1x iPad Spotlight iOS 7 40pt:	**AppIcon40x40.png**
2x iPad Spotlight iOS 7 40pt:	**AppIcon40x40@2x.png**
1x iPad App iOS 7 76pt:	**AppIcon76x76.png**
2x iPad App iOS 7 76pt:	**AppIcon76x76@2x.png**

14. When we add images using the assets catalog, the files are automatically copied over to the project folder. Let's take a look. In the Project Navigator, **Right–click** on **Images.xcassets** and choose **Show in Finder**. This reveals the folder in the Finder.

15. Go into the **Images.xcassets** folder.

16. Go into the **AppIcon.appiconset** folder and notice all our icon images have been copied into this folder. Sweet!

17. Switch back to Xcode. Let's test the icons in the iOS Simulator. Set the active **Scheme** (top left of the window) to **iPhone Retina (4-inch).**

18. Click the **Run** button (▶) and hit **Stop** if a warning appears.

19. In the iOS Simulator, go to **Hardware > Home** so you can see the new custom icon!

20. Switch back to Xcode.

ADDING THE LAUNCH IMAGES

Now we need to add the launch images for the app. This is a similar process as the app icons, but the launch images have their own catalog.

1. In the Editor, click the **LaunchImage** catalog in the column on the left.

App Settings: Icons & Launch Images INTRO TO iOS

2. In the **Attributes inspector** tab ( ), notice that in the **iOS 7.0 and Later** section, **iPhone Portrait** is checked. We also need to add launch images for Landscape on the iPad, so let's check those options.

3. Check on **Landscape** for the **iPad** to add areas for those launch images in the asset catalog.

   Unlike the app icons, the sizes are not listed below. Luckily you can click on any of the empty launch image areas to see the required sizes in the **Attributes inspector** tab ( ).

4. Click on the first empty launch image area (2x iPhone Portrait iOS 7) to select it.

5. At the bottom of the **Attributes inspector** tab ( ), notice next to Expected Size, it says **640 x 960 pixels.**

6. Click on the second empty launch image area (R4 iPhone Portrait iOS 7) to select it.

   NOTE: R4 stands for Retina 4-inch.

7. At the bottom of the **Attributes inspector** tab ( ), notice next to Expected Size, it says **640 x 1136 pixels.** Sweet! Let's add our launch images.

8. Open a Finder window.

9. Navigate to the **Desktop > Class Files > yourname-iOS Intro Class > App Launch Images** folder.

10. Position the Finder window so you can see it as well as the empty launch image areas in Xcode.

11. From the Finder window, drag the **Default@2x-iphone.png** file over to Xcode and drop it over the empty **2x iPhone Portrait iOS 7** launch image area.

12. Repeat this process for the rest of the app icons, dragging over the corresponding files:

    R4 iPhone Portrait iOS 7:   **Default@2x-iphone-r4.png**
    1x iPad Landscape iOS 7:   **Default-Landscape-ipad.png**
    2x iPad Landscape iOS 7:   **Default-Landscape@2x-ipad.png**

TESTING THE LAUNCH IMAGES

Our app launches quickly, so the launch image will not be displayed for very long. But let's try to see it, so we can make sure it's working. Our iPhone's launch image is shown to the right. That's what you'll be looking for as the app loads. It will only be visible for a moment, and then the bands table will load. You'll have to watch closely or you'll miss it!

1. Click the **Run** button ( ) and click **Stop** if a warning appears.

PAGE 172   INTRO TO iPHONE/iPAD APP DEVELOPMENT

INTRO TO iOS *App Settings: Icons & Launch Images*

6D EXERCISE

2. Did you see it? If it happened too fast, switch back to Xcode and click the **Run** button (▶) again.

   NOTE: The launch image is only shown when the app launches from a fresh state. If you leave the app by hitting the Home button, when you go back into the app it will often be reloaded from a saved state. Therefore the launch image may not be displayed. You must start the app fresh to be able to see the launch image. Running the app again will ensure that.

3. Switch back to Xcode.

4. In the Project Navigator, click on **Main_iPad.storyboard**.

5. Go to **File > Save**.

ADDING ITUNESARTWORK FILES

The next two files are optional and are only used for Ad Hoc distribution. When developing an app you'll want to send it to testers to work out all the kinks and bugs before submitting it to the app store. This is known as Ad Hoc distribution. These files are used in the App list in iTunes, and it is recommended you add them for Ad Hoc distribution so testers get the full experience of the app. If you do not include them, they will just see a blank icon in the App list. These files should not be included in the project for the final submission to the App store.

1. These two files need to be added directly into the **Jive Factory** root folder. In the Project Navigator, click on the **Jive Factory** project name.

2. Go to **File > Add Files to "Jive Factory"**.

3. Navigate to the **Desktop,** then go to **Class Files > yourname-iOS Intro Class > iTunesArtwork Files.**

4. Press **Cmd–A** to select all the images in that folder.

5. At the bottom of the window, set the following:

        Destination: Check **Copy items into destination group's folder (if needed)**
              Folders: No folders are being added, so leave as is.
       Add to targets: Check on **Jive Factory**

6. Click the **Add** button.

7. Notice we just added two **iTunesArtwork** files. Take careful notice of the file names. Unlike the other images we added in this exercise, these files have to follow these naming conventions. That's all that's necessary for these two files.

App Settings: Icons & Launch Images INTRO TO iOS

To keep things organized let's move these two files to the **Supporting Files** folder.

8. In the Project Navigator, click on one of the **iTunesArtwork** files then **Shift–click** on the other to select them both.

9. Drag them into the **Supporting Files** folder.

   NOTE: Even though we ended up moving the files into the **Supporting Files** folder in Xcode, adding them into the main project folder and then moving them into Supporting Files is different than importing them directly into Supporting Files! These files still reside in the Jive Factory root folder (which you can confirm by looking in the Finder).

   Congratulations, this app is done!

CHANGING THE NAME OF THE APP

When first creating a project, you choose a project name. This is used for the app name. You may need to change this later. For example, once you see that name on the Home Screen, you may realize it's too long and the name is being shortened with an ellipse (...) in the middle. To rename a project:

1. In the Project Navigator, click on the project name to select it.
2. Click again on the project name and pause for a moment until the name becomes editable. Enter a new name and hit **Return**.
3. When asked about renaming the project content items, click **Rename**.
4. When asked about snapshots, click **Enable**.
5. When it's done, click **OK**.

REFERENCE MATERIAL

Check Out
OUR OTHER WORKBOOKS!

- Web Development
- JavaScript & jQuery
- GreenSock Animation
- HTML5 & CSS3
- Mobile & Responsive Web Design
- WordPress.org
- WordPress.com
- PHP & MySQL
- Ruby on Rails

- HTML Email
- Using Real Fonts on the Web
- Adobe Dreamweaver
- Adobe Fireworks
- Intro to Objective-C
- Intro to iPhone/iPad App Development
- Adobe CC: Intro to InDesign, Photoshop, & Illustrator

- Adobe InDesign
- Digital Publishing Suite
- eBooks with InDesign
- Adobe Illustrator
- Adobe Photoshop
- Photoshop Advanced
- Photoshop Elements
- Adobe Lightroom
- Adobe After Effects

NOBLEDESKTOP.COM/BOOKS

INTRO TO iOS *Submitting to the App Store*

REFERENCE

APP STORE SUBMISSION OVERVIEW

This reference guide provides you with a summary of the steps involved in submitting an app to the Apple App Store. Apple provides detailed steps for submitting your app to their App Store on their developer website in their app distribution guide. We'll direct you to the appropriate parts of Apple's guide as we summarize the process for you, but you can always read Apple's full documentation on their website here:

tinyurl.com/app-distribution-guide

There are five main administrative tasks for submitting an app to the App Store.

- Enrolling in the iOS Developer Program
- Provisioning Your Device For Testing and Deployment
- Creating an iTunes Record
- Submitting Your App
- Releasing Your App

ENROLLING IN THE iOS DEVELOPER PROGRAM

To put your app on the App Store, you need to join the iOS Developer program, which costs $99 USD per year. Follow the steps below to see the instructions for adding your account to Xcode on Apple's website. If you have not already joined the iOS Developer program, don't worry you can join the program in Xcode.

1. Open your favorite web browser (Safari, Chrome, Firefox, etc.).

2. Go to **tinyurl.com/app-distribution-guide**

3. On the left, expand **Managing Accounts.**

4. Click on **Adding Your Apple ID Account in Xcode.**

5. On the right, click on **To add an Apple ID account** to expand that section.

6. Follow the steps to add your account to Xcode and enroll in the iOS Developer program if you haven't already.

7. Here are a few things to keep in mind:

   – You can use your existing Apple ID that you use for iTunes, or you can create a new ID if you wish to keep your professional and personal accounts separate.
   – You will be asked if you want to enroll as an individual or company. Most of you will choose individual unless you are part of a larger company that is paying for the license. If you are enrolling as a company, you will need to submit additional paperwork, which Apple lists for you during the enrollment process.

Submitting to the App Store INTRO TO iOS

- You will be asked to enter your billing information for identity verification. You won't be asked for a credit card yet, but you should enter your name as it appears on the credit card you are using and the billing address on the credit card.
- Make sure you select the iOS Developer program. This is $99/year.
- After you complete your purchase, you will receive a confirmation email from the Apple Online Store.
- It will take a day or so for Apple to process your order, after which you will receive an activation email from Apple Developer Program Support. Once you click the activation link in that email, you are ready for the next part of submitting your app to the App Store.

PROVISIONING YOUR DEVICE FOR TESTING AND DEPLOYMENT

As you develop your iOS apps, you will use the iOS Simulator to test the apps during most of the development process. However, you must test your app on an actual iPhone, iPad, or iPod touch before you publish to the App Store. In addition, some features may not work on the simulator.

All iOS apps must be code signed and provisioned (prepared and configured to launch on devices). You can do all this in Xcode once you have an iOS Developer account. For detailed steps on testing your app on devices follow these steps to get to the appropriate section of Apple's Documentation.

1. Open your favorite web browser (Safari, Chrome, Firefox, etc.).
2. Go to **tinyurl.com/app-distribuition-guide**
3. On the left, click on **Configuring Your Xcode Project for Distribution** section.
4. Follow the steps in this section to configure your project settings and create a provisioning profile.
5. Once you have your provisioning profile set-up, go back to the app distribution guide: **tinyurl.com/app-distribuition-guide**
6. On the left click on **Launching Your App on Devices** for steps on testing on your device.

Once you've tested your app on your device, you'll also want to test it out on as many devices as possible, under real world conditions. To test your app on a variety of devices, you need to create a special distribution provisioning profile, called an Ad Hoc provisioning profile. Once you have that you need to send it, along with the app, to testers. With an Ad Hoc provisioning profile, testers do not need to be enrolled in an Apple Developer Program. They do not need to be added to your team. They do not need to create signing certificates. They do not need Xcode to run your app. Testers simply install the app and the Ad Hoc provisioning profile on their device using iTunes. They are then able to use the app on their devices, and you are able to collect and analyze crash reports or logs from these testers to resolve problems before shipping your app.

INTRO TO iOS *Submitting to the App Store*

7. Go back to the app distribution guide: **tinyurl.com/app-distribuition-guide**

8. On the left, click on **Beta Testing Your iOS App.**

9. Follow the steps to create an Ad Hoc provisioning profile and send your app to testers.

CREATING AN iTUNES RECORD

When you purchase an app from the App Store, you've probably noticed that there is a lot of information on the app page: app icon, screenshots of the app, app name, description, company info, etc. You provide this information when you create a record for the app in the iTunes Connect portal. You have to do this before submitting your app to Apple. (It is also recommended that you do this before beta testing a final candidate for a release so that you can validate the app before sending it out to testers.)

Usually, you would create an iTunes record late in the development process because there's a time limit from when you create the record to when you must submit your app. Some Apple technologies, like Game Center and In-App Purchase, require that an iTunes Connect record be created before the development process is complete so that you can test the code you added to implement these technologies.

1. Open your favorite web browser (Safari, Chrome, Firefox, etc.).

2. Go to **tinyurl.com/creating-app-record**

3. Follow the steps to create an iTunes record for your app.

SUBMITTING YOUR APP

Once you have tested the app and resolved any issues your testers may have had, you are ready to submit your app to the App Store. There are several steps to doing this. To start, you have to create a store distribution provisioning profile using Member Center.

Member Center is where you manage your account and access resources and benefits included with your Developer Program membership. You can sign into Member Center here: **developer.apple.com/membercenter**

With a distribution provisioning profile created, you can then use Xcode to archive, validate, and submit your working app to the App Store.

1. Open your favorite web browser (Safari, Chrome, Firefox, etc.).

2. Go to **tinyurl.com/app-distribution-guide**

3. On the left, click on **Submitting Your App.**

Submitting to the App Store INTRO TO iOS

4. Follow the steps to submit your app to the App Store for approval.

   Once your app has been submitted, Apple will review your app to make sure it conforms to their app guidelines. For information on those guidelines check out the following links:

   tinyurl.com/ios7-ui-guidelines
   tinyurl.com/iosappguidelines

RELEASING THE APP

Once your app has been approved, all that's left to do is set the date you want your app to be available to customers using iTunes Connect. For steps on releasing your app:

1. Open your favorite web browser (Safari, Chrome, Firefox, etc.).

2. Go to **tinyurl.com/app-distribution-guide**

3. On the left, expand **Managing Your App in iTunes Connect.**

4. Click on **Changing the Availability Date of Your App.**

5. On the right under **Changing the Availability Date of Your App** click on **To set the availability date** to expand it.

6. Follow the steps given to release your app.

7. Once the app is released, you will have to update, fix and do other maintenance tasks. For an overview of these tasks, go back to the app distribution guide: **tinyurl.com/app-distribuition-guide**

8. On the left, click on **Releasing and Updating Your App.**

INTRO TO iOS *App Icon & Launch Image File Names & Sizes*

REFERENCE

We couldn't find a single perfect source (that was easy to understand) with this information. So here is all the important info in one easy-to-reference place.

DEVICE/SCREEN	RECOMMENDED FILE NAMES	SIZE IN PIXELS
iPhone & iPod Touch		
App Icon	Icon60x60@2x.png	120 x 120
Spotlight Icon	Icon40x40@2x.png	80 x 80
Settings Icon	Icon29x29@2x.png	58 x 58
Launch Image Portrait Retina 4-inch	Default@2x-iphone-r4.png	640 x 1136
Launch Image Portrait Retina 3.5-inch	Default@2x-iphone.png	640 x 960
iPad		
App Icon (Retina display)	Icon72x72@2x.png	152 x 152
App Icon	Icon72x72.png	76 x 76
Spotlight Icon (Retina display)	Icon40x40@2x.png	80 x 80
Spotlight Icon	Icon40x40.png	40 x 40
Settings Icon (Retina display)	Icon29x29@2x.png	58 x 58
Settings Icon	Icon29x29.png	29 x 29
Launch Image Portrait (Retina display)	Default-Portrait@2x-ipad.png	1536 x 2048
Launch Image Portrait	Default-Portrait-ipad.png	768 x 1024
Launch Image Landscape (Retina display)	Default-Landscape@2x-ipad.png	2048 x 1536
Launch Image Landscape	Default-Landscape-ipad.png	1024 x 768

ITUNES	REQUIRED FILE NAMES	SIZE IN PIXELS
App Icon for iTunes (Retina display) Only needs to be added into the app for Ad Hoc distribution (private app testing).	iTunesArtwork@2x Must be a PNG, but do not add file extension to the name	1024 x 1024
App Icon for iTunes Only needs to be added into the app for Ad Hoc distribution (private app testing). Will be needed when submitting the final app on Apple's website.	iTunesArtwork Must be a PNG, but do not add file extension to the name	512 x 512

INTRO TO iOS *Objective-C Programming: Basic Terms & Concepts*

REFERENCE

OBJECTIVE-C

The primary programming language used to write apps for OS X and iOS.

OBJECT-ORIENTED PROGRAMMING

Objective-C is an object-oriented programming language. Object-Oriented programming is a programming paradigm (style of programming) that represents concepts as objects that have data fields (attributes that describe the object) known as properties and associated procedures (behaviors) known as methods. Objects are used to interact with one another to design applications and computer programs.

Traditional, non-object-oriented programming is generally linear and not very reusable. It is also difficult to assign meaningful connections between different parts of the code. As a result, the more code there is, the more of a maintenance nightmare it becomes. That's why object-oriented programming was created.

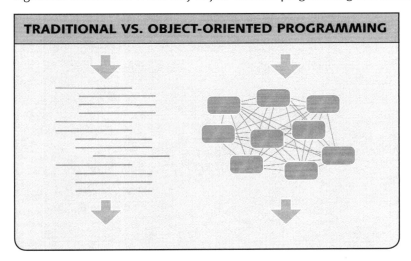

OBJECTS

An object in object-oriented programming isn't that different from an object in real life. In the real world, an object is a tangible and visible thing, like a house, car or person.

In object-oriented programming an object is used to represent things in your program, such as the visual buttons or text fields in a contacts app.

Objects are created from classes. The graphic on the right shows eight objects in a typical contacts app. These eight objects were created from two classes: UITextField and UIButton.

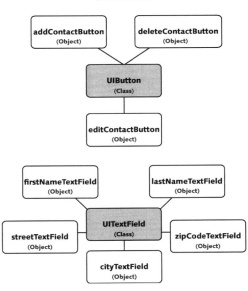

NOBLE DESKTOP — STEP BY STEP TRAINING — NOBLEDESKTOP.COM

Objective-C Programming: Basic Terms & Concepts INTRO TO iOS

REFERENCE

CLASS

The blueprint or template for an object. Objects are instances of classes. A class defines how objects look and what they do. In the real world, there are hundreds of Toyota Camry cars (objects), but they are all based on the Camry design (class).

A class consists of two files: a header file (.h) and an implementation file (.m).

SOME COMMON CLASSES

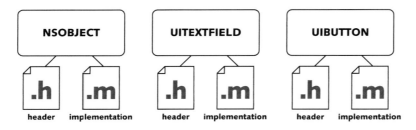

INSTANTIATION

Instantiation means to create an instance of a class (bringing it to life), by allocating memory to it and initializing it. Writing a class is the first part of creating an object. Once you write a class you still need to create an object from that class in your program. This process is known as instantiation. Below is typical code for creating an object (an instance of your class).

INSTANTIATION

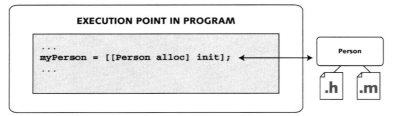

The code above instantiates a new object called myPerson. myPerson is an instance of our Person class. The double arrow illustrates the connection between our myPerson object and the Person class.

SUBCLASS

A class that inherits its properties and behavior from another class. When creating classes you'll often want the class to inherit the behavior of other classes that have already been written for you. This way your object has all the properties and behavior of an existing class, but you can add your own specific properties and behaviors to enhance it. Apple provides you with many existing classes for common objects in all programs, such as buttons and labels. By making your own button and label a subclass of existing buttons and labels, you save yourself from having to program the basic functionality of a button over again, and can focus on programming what makes it unique from the standard button. Why reinvent the wheel when you don't have to?

INTRO TO iOS *Objective-C Programming: Basic Terms & Concepts*

REFERENCE

The graphic below shows that **UIButton** is a subclass of **UIControl,** which is a subclass of **UIView,** and so on. You can see that each time a new subclass is made it gets more and more functionality (properties and behavior from its parent class).

INHERITANCE

HEADER FILE (.h)

One of the two files that make up a class. It contains only the declarations of properties and methods for the class. It does NOT contain any programming logic that specifically defines what the methods or properties do within the program, it just lists the properties and methods the class has. Think of it as a table of contents, which defines the properties and methods for a class. The .h file exposes a list of methods for other classes to use, without including the intricacies of those methods.

IMPLEMENTATION FILE (.m)

One of the two files that make up a class. It contains the programming logic that specifically defines what the methods or properties do within the program. Below is an example of an empty Person class:

EMPTY CLASS

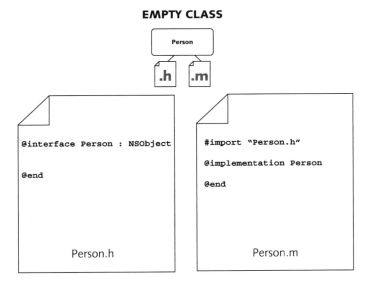

When you create a new class in Xcode, these two files are automatically created for you. In the Person.h file, you declare properties and methods between the @interface and @end lines. In the Person.m file, you add all the programming logic for your methods between the @implementation and @end lines.

Objective-C Programming: Basic Terms & Concepts   INTRO TO iOS

PROPERTY

Properties represents the characteristics of an object. For example, in the real world cars are a specific color, have a specific type of engine, etc. In the example in the graphic below, our Person class has two properties defined: firstName and lastName.

CLASS WITH PROPERTIES DEFINED

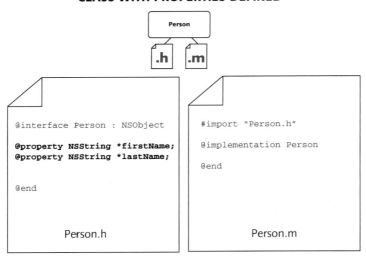

METHOD

A procedure. Methods define the behavior of an object. For example, in the real world, a car drives from point A to point B. In our Person class below, we've added a method. Notice that in the header file (Person.h) we declare the method, but add all the programming logic for that method in our implementation file (Person.m). The sayHello method doesn't do anything too complicated. It uses NSLog to display the text "Hello, world!" in the Xcode console.

CLASS WITH METHOD ADDED

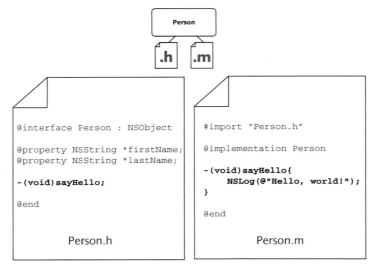

INTRO TO iOS *Objective-C Programming: Basic Terms & Concepts*

REFERENCE

METHOD SYNTAX AND MESSAGING

Methods in Objective-C have a specific syntax:

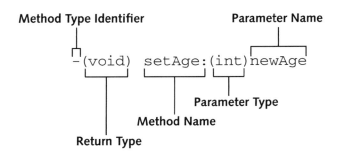

- It starts with the method type identifier, either a **dash (-)** or a **plus sign (+)**. There are two kinds of methods in Objective-C: **instance methods (-)** and **class methods (+)**.
- **(void)** is the return type. This method doesn't have a return type (that's why it's void), but methods can return any type (primitive, object, class, etc.).
- Next is the name of the method, which in this case is **setAge:**
- After that is the parameter for the method. The parameter consists of the parameter type, in this case it is an integer, and the parameter name, newAge. While the example above has only one parameter, a method can have multiple parameters, or no parameters at all.

The graphic below gives a visual demonstration of a method with no parameters in action. It demonstrates how one part of the program messages another to complete a task.

BASIC MESSAGING PROGRAM FLOW

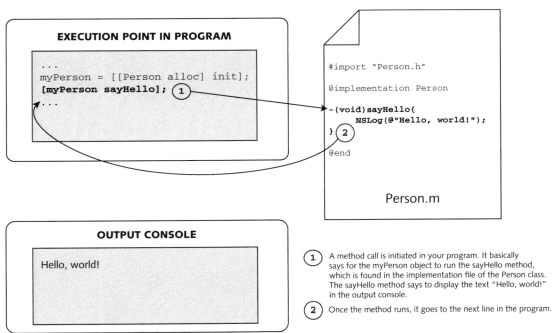

① A method call is initiated in your program. It basically says for the myPerson object to run the sayHello method, which is found in the implementation file of the Person class. The sayHello method says to display the text "Hello, world!" in the output console.

② Once the method runs, it goes to the next line in the program.

Objective-C Programming: Basic Terms & Concepts INTRO TO iOS

INSTANCE METHOD

An instance method is a method whose execution is scoped to a particular instance of the class. In other words, before you call an instance method, you must first create an instance of the class. Instance methods are the most common type of method.

CLASS METHOD

A class method is a method whose execution is scoped to the method's class. It does not require an instance of an object to be the receiver of a message. You often use class methods either as factory methods to create new instances of the class or to access some piece of shared information associated with the class. For example, when instantiating an object, you use the class method alloc.

ACCESSOR METHODS

Accessor methods get and set the state or value of an object. For example, let's say you have a light bulb object in your app. This object can either be on or off. To determine if that light bulb object is on or off, you would use an accessor method called a getter. If you want to set that object to be off, you would use an accessor method called a setter to set the object to off.

Another example would be if we add an age property to our Person class:

AGE PROPERTY DEFINED

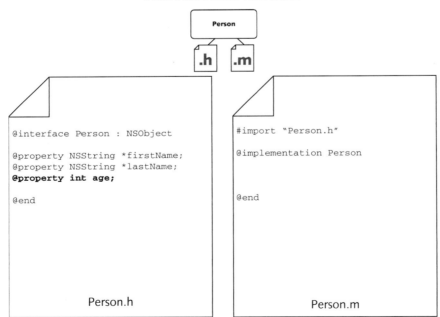

PAGE 188   INTRO TO iPHONE/iPAD APP DEVELOPMENT

INTRO TO iOS *Objective-C Programming: Basic Terms & Concepts*

REFERENCE

To find out the age of our Person objects or set the age on one of our Person objects, we need to use what are called getter and setter methods (shown below). With these methods we can access the age property (be able to get the age of our myPerson object or set the age of our myPerson object):

GETTER AND SETTER METHODS

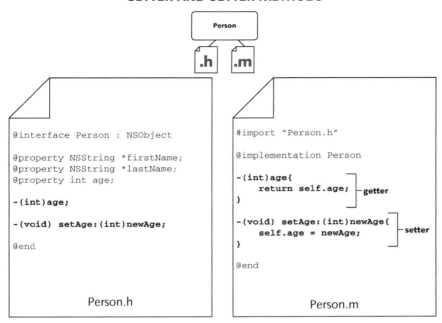

Although we must use getters and setters to access our properties, we no longer have to write them ourselves. Over the years, this part of programming became such a common and arduous practice that the Objective-C language was changed to create these methods when the code is compiled.

Starting with Xcode 4.4, getter and setter methods are automatically created for you by the compiler when you define a property. While it's good to know how getter and setter methods are written, you don't have to write them to be able to use properties!

PARAMETERS

A parameter is a value you are giving to the method. Methods sometimes require specific information. You send that info to it as a parameter.

Objective-C Programming: Basic Terms & Concepts INTRO TO iOS

Below is an example of the code for a method that takes a parameter.

METHOD WITH PARAMETER

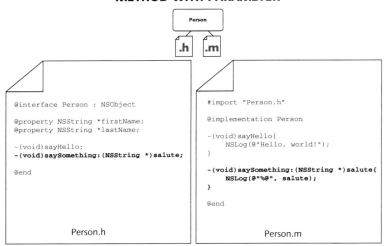

In the graphic below you can see how the method works in our program and how the parameter gets passed within our method.

BASIC MESSAGING PROGRAM FLOW WITH METHOD WITH PARAMETER

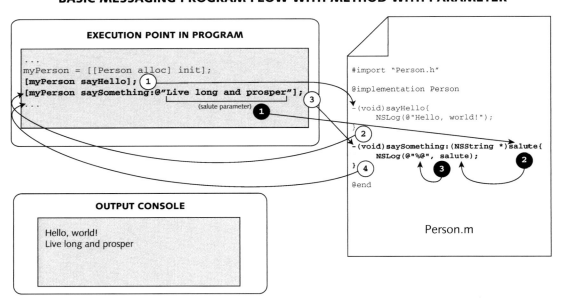

METHOD FLOW

1. The sayHello method is called on the myPerson object. It displays "Hello, world!" in the output console.
2. The program goes to the next line of code.
3. The saySomething: method is called on the myPerson object. The text "Live long and prosper" (a parameter) is passed along to the method in the Person class. The saySomething: method says to display this text in the output console.
4. The program goes to the next line of code.

PARAMETER FLOW

1. The saySomething: method requires an NSString parameter. We pass along the text "Live long and prosper" as the parameter.
2. The salute parameter (Live long and prosper) is called by NSLog.
3. The salute parameter (Live long and prosper) replaces the %@.

PAGE 190   INTRO TO iPHONE/iPAD APP DEVELOPMENT

INTRO TO iOS *Objective-C Programming: Basic Terms & Concepts*

REFERENCE

PROTOCOLS

Protocols are an agreement that a class adheres to. Think of them as contracts. When you use a protocol in your class, you are basically saying that your class has to do everything that the protocol states.

DELEGATE

A delegate is a protocol that defines a set of methods that a class should implement. In the real world, you often have projects that you need to complete for work. However, you yourself don't always have to do everything to complete that tasks. Often, you are able to delegate, or push some of that work to someone else. That's essentially what a class does with a delegate.

For a real world example, a bride is tasked with planning a wedding. While she can do all the work herself, she can also delegate some of that work to a wedding planner. In this case the wedding planner becomes the delegate. She is tasked with getting certain tasks done, and the bride doesn't have to worry about doing them.

DATA SOURCE

A data source is like a delegate except that, instead of being delegated tasks to complete, it is delegated control of data. There are some classes that need specific data to complete their task. For example, a table view (displays a table) needs to know how many rows to draw and what information it should populate those rows with. This information comes from a data source.

FURTHER READING

You can find more information on programming with Objective-C on Apple's website:

tinyurl.com/oop-with-objective-c

tinyurl.com/programming-objective-c